DESIGNED BY GOD

Books in this series—

DESIGNED BY GOD

A Woman's Workshop on Wholeness

Kirkie Morrissey

Lamplighter Books Grand Rapids, Michigan
Zondervan Publishing House

DESIGNED BY GOD
Copyright © 1985 by The Zondervan Corporation
Grand Rapids, Michigan

Lamplighter Books are published by Zondervan
Publishing House, 1415 Lake Drive, S.E.,
Grand Rapids, Michigan 49506

Library of Congress Cataloging in Publication Data

Morrissey, Kirkie.
    Designed by God.
    1. Spiritual exercises.   2. Christian life—1960–
3. Gifts, Spiritual.   I. Title.
BV4509.5.M68   1984   248.4   84-23460
ISBN 0-310-45011-X

Printed in the United States of America

88   89   90   91   92   93   94 / CH / 12   11   10   9   8   7   6   5

Mom and Dad,
with love—and with thanks for
being God's instruments in giving me life

CONTENTS

ACKNOWLEDGMENTS

I would like to thank my dear friend Nancy Metz for her time, effort, and skill in reviewing this manuscript. Her willing spirit has been a joy, and her insights helpful. I thank her, too, for her faithfulness in prayer with me as the Lord laid this Bible study on our hearts.

Also, I would like to express my deep appreciation to the women who participated in this study in Colorado Springs and to each leader who facilitated those groups. Their input, encouragement, and friendship has meant a great deal to me. It has been exciting to see how the Lord has touched hearts and transformed lives through this study of His Word.

I thank, too, my dear husband, Terry; and our special boys, Scott, Reid, and Mark. Their loving support, affirmation, and prayers have enabled me to complete this task.

Also, I extend my thanks to my editor at Zondervan, Janet Kobobel. She is a delight to work with, and her skill and dedication are much appreciated.

May the Lord be revealed, honored, and glorified through this study. It is out of love for Him and joy in walking with Him that this is written. To Him be the praise.

INTRODUCTION

In the parable of the talents in Matthew 25, Jesus commended two individuals for what they had done with all that had been entrusted to them. As they had been faithful with what they had been given, they were praised with a "well done." Then they were rewarded and invited to share the joy of their master. How exciting! There was another individual, however, who out of fear had buried that which had been entrusted to him. . . .

This parable can be interpreted to represent our lives. Each of us has been entrusted with one life. For living this life, each has been given certain gifts, capabilities, and abilities. The Lord of Life has a design for each of us to become all we were created to be. Yet, for various reasons, we may choose not to risk, not to "go for it." We "bury" ourselves, remaining safe. However, the Lord has such abundant life and joy planned for us! As we are faithful with what He has entrusted to us, how exciting it will be to receive His "well done."

To help you become all God designed you to be, the Lord has provided His Word, the Bible. In this He reveals Himself to you. He speaks to you, ministers to you, and guides you. As you do this study, let Him be your Teacher. Before you begin each day, pray. Ask Him to work within you. It is the Lord who heals, molds, and gives growth. He brings wholeness. Therefore, it is important to open yourself to Him.

To benefit most fully from this study, it is important to spend time each day working on it. To help you in this, each chapter is apportioned into daily segments. Assignments are given, also, which are *key* in enabling the truths to become an integral part of your life and your being. To receive the fullest benefit, the assignments must be done! (You may also want to use this study with a group. The sharing of discoveries and mutual accountability among friends can be helpful.)

An integral part of each lesson is assignments for you to do in a separate notebook. This notebook will become your journal, your chronicle of how you grow as you complete each lesson. This study/journal is divided into two parts. The first deals with "inner healing," considering things that can keep you from wholeness (such as a poor self-image, deep hurts, anger, guilt.) The second half delves into actualizing your God-given potential (such as the plans He has for you, the specific works He has prepared, the spiritual gifts He has given you, and freedom from disabling fear). The result is wholeness, living in the process and joy of becoming all God created *you* to be!

You will be amazed at the person you can become; for God "is able to do immeasurably more than all we ask or imagine, according to his power that is at work within us." Now "to him be glory in the church and in Christ Jesus

throughout all generations, for ever and ever! Amen."
(Ephesians 3:21 NIV)*

---

*This study was prepared using the *New International Version* of the Bible. It is recommended for your use as you delve into God's Word.

Part I

Experiencing Inner Healing

1

IS THERE ANYONE WHO KNOWS WHO I AM?

Here I am. But who am I? Why am I here? Did I just happen? Am I on my own with this puzzle? Or is there someone who knows the answers to my questions—and who knows me, as I am today, with all the changes that have taken place in me since I was born?

As you begin your journal and study the Scriptures, be honest with your feelings and your questions. *Keep bringing them before the Lord.* In His Word God promises: "Ask and it will be given to you; seek and you will find; knock and the door will be opened to you. For *everyone* who asks receives; he who seeks finds; and to him who knocks, the door will be opened" (Matthew 7:7–8 [italics mine]). The Lord also promises that when you call to Him, He *will* answer you and will tell you great and unsearchable things you presently do not know (Jeremiah 33:3 [italics mine]). God is faithful, and He will guide you into all truth.

(DAY 1) Exploring the Question "Did I Just Happen?"

1. Respond to this statement: Up to this point my life has seemed. . . (Check as many as are applicable.)

_____ Meaningless.

_____ Confusing.

_____ To have some purpose.

_____ Very meaningful.

2. Check the statements that best complete this sentence: I have felt that for myself. . .

_____ I was not wanted here.

_____ I do not belong in this world.

_____ I am a mistake.

_____ I definately belong.

_____ I was created specially by God.

_____ I was designed for God's purpose.

3. Turn to God's Word and record phrases from the following verses which give you insight into whether or not you "just happened."

Psalm 119:73 _____

Psalm 139:13–16 _____

Isaiah 43:1 _____

Isaiah 44:24 _____

Isaiah 46:3 _____

4. In a separate notebook record your thoughts and feelings after reading these passages:

Thoughts   *Feelings*

5. ASSIGNMENT: Write your name in the blank below. Repeat the sentence to yourself, emphasizing a different word each time you repeat it. Throughout this week continue to repeat this truth every time you look in the mirror. "God created me, _____, special—just as He wanted me to be!"

6. ASSIGNMENT: Write out a verse from question 3 and commit it to memory. Meditate on this verse throughout the week. (Each week there will be a verse to memorize. The verse will help "root" these truths in your heart. You may want to put your memory verses on 3x5 cards for easy review.)

(DAY 2) Exploring the Question "How Well Am I Known?—1

7. You might wonder if God still knows you, for you have changed a lot since you were created! Describe how well you think God knows you today. Be specific. _____

_____

_____

8. What insight do the following verses give you?

Psalm 44:21 _____

Jeremiah 17:10 _____

Ezekiel 11:5 _____

Matthew 10:30 _____

1 John 3:20 _____

9. ASSIGNMENT: As you experience various, specific feelings this week, note what they are, and consciously remind yourself, "God knows what I'm feeling. He understands."

(DAY 3) Exploring the Question "How Well Am I Known?" — 2

10. Read Psalm 139:1–4. In your notebook write this passage out in your own words, applying it specifically to yourself at this moment. For example: Verse 2—"Lord, you are aware of me sitting in this chair right now. You know and understand what I am thinking about my circumstances (my job, my marriage, my children, my financial situation, etc.). You know how I am feeling about myself (that I'm so loved by You; or I'm feeling fat, undisciplined, and unlovable; or I'm feeling lonely or guilty). And Lord, you know how I'm struggling to know who I am and what my purpose is in being here." As you follow each verse in this passage, write your own expression as specifically and personally as possible.

11. Complete this sentence: Realizing how completely and intimately God knows me, I feel _____

12. Respond specifically to this statement: Discovering how well He knows me helps me today in the following ways:

With my feelings:

With my thoughts:

With my circumstances:

With my tasks:

With my problems:

In my relationship with the Lord:

And especially today in . . .

13. Describe the expectation you have now to discover who you are. Give your reasons. _____

_____

_____

(DAY 4) Exploring How Well God Knows Me as Exhibited by Jesus Christ

14. Jesus Christ is God Incarnate; God in the flesh! (See John 1:1, 14; Colossians 1:15–20; and Hebrews 1:3.) Therefore, the discoveries you made above can be documented by examining Christ's awareness of people as He walked on this earth.

a. In the incident recorded in Matthew 9:1–8, what phrase reveals His knowledge of what is going on within us?

_____

_____

b. Describe how this is portrayed in Mark 2:8 _____

_____

c. Record a similar phrase from the incident described in Luke 9:46–48. _____

d. What does Jesus' dialogue with Nathanael in John 1:45–51 reveal? _____

_____

15. If Christ were to come up to you today He might say: __

_____

16. ASSIGNMENT: Visualize Jesus approaching you throughout the day in your tasks and when you are aware of specific feelings or struggles. Open yourself to His help. Record in your journal what happens as you do this.

(DAY 5) Exploring God's Acceptance of Me

17. Since God knows you so completely, do you think He can accept you? _____
Express your fears and questions in your notebook.

18. From the following passages record the insights you receive:

a. Read John 4:1−29. List those things which indicate Jesus' acceptance of the Samaritan woman. _____

_____

_____

b. What is Jesus' attitude toward the woman caught in adultery in John 8:1−11? _____

_____

c. How does Jesus respond to Thomas in his doubt in John 20:24−28?

_____

19. Read Jesus' encounter with Zacchaeus, the tax collector, in Luke 19:1−10. How does it encourage you that Jesus went "to be the guest of a 'sinner'" and that He came "to seek and to save what was lost"? _____

_____

20. Complete this sentence in your journal: Exploring how Jesus Christ dealt with people helps me in the following ways:

21. Record your thoughts in your journal on this statement: Realizing God's total awareness (along with His acceptance) of me, frees me in the following ways:

Personal Reflection (record in your notebook):

1. This week I've explored how the Lord created me special and today knows my every thought, is aware of each emotion I experience, and sees every act I do, and everything that happens to me. As I've concentrated on these truths I've noticed the following things within myself:

2. My relationship with God is beginning to change in the following ways:

3. I would like to continue to grow in the following areas: (Review weekly.)

2

THE FIRST STEP TOWARD WHOLENESS

How wonderful to discover there is One who knows you completely.

How comforting to realize that this One who knows you also accepts you as you are.

How exciting to have hope for becoming all you were created to be.

To experience God's resources in and for your life, do you wonder if there is anything you need to do? Are you already linked to God's power? Or do you need to establish the connection? Perhaps you have already done this but feel you need recharging. Do you struggle with your own nature and wonder why you are the way you are? Do you feel alone in your struggles? For help and insight into these matters, turn to God's Word. (If you question the validity of the Bible, read John R. W. Stott's pamphlet "The Authority of the Bible.")

(DAY 1) Exploring Our Natural Condition

1. What problems do you see in our world today? _____

_____

_____

2. Have such problems always existed? Explain. _____

_____

_____

3. I think these problems exist because: _____

_____

_____

4. The Bible speaks to these issues. Read Romans 5:12–19; Galatians 5:16–24; and Ephesians 2:1–10.

a. What entered the world after God had created it good (Romans 5:12)? _____

b. What are the results of this sinful nature we now *all* have (Galatians 5:19-21)? _____

c. Spiritually, what is our condition apart from Jesus Christ (Ephesians 2:1)? _____

d. What personal insights have you received from these passages? _____

e. What are your reactions or responses to these discoveries? _____

5. If, in fact, the above discoveries are true, what effect would this have on your wholeness as an individual? _____

_____

6. Check the statement that expresses your feelings: I feel the Biblical explanation of the condition and basic nature of man is:

_____ *Right on!*   _____ *Way off*   _____*Worth considering*

7. Complete this statement: The questions I have are:

(DAY 2) Exploring Evidences of This Nature

8. Are there ever times when you're surprised by what you're thinking? Are you ever shocked at or embarrassed by your actions or reactions? If so, you're not alone!

a. What does the Apostle Paul reveal of his basic nature in Romans 7:15–19? _____

_____

b. How did the great King David share Paul's struggles? Read 2 Samuel 11:2–5, 14-17. _____

_____

c. Abraham, the "Father of our Faith," also gives evidence of this basic nature in Genesis 12:10–13. What does Abraham (Abram) do here? _____

_____

9. Record in your journal the struggles you have with your basic nature.

     I Want to Do   *But Sometimes I Do*

10. Write out in your notebook what you have learned from chapter 1 that's encouraging to you.

11. Complete this statement in your journal: Understanding the reasons why I am the way I am and why the world is the way it is helps me in the following ways:

12. ASSIGNMENT: List in your notebook experiences (hurts, disappointments) from your own life which support the scriptural insights on mankind's basic nature. Also, list other evidence you observe in situations around you.

     Experiences   *Observations*

(DAY 3) Exploring Jesus' Teaching on What We Need

13. Why do you think the Bible bothers to expose and explain these problems and the negative condition of man? __

_____

14. Do you think there's hope for you and for mankind—a solution to our problems? _____
What do you discover regarding a solution from God's Word in Proverbs 2:1–10; John 5:39–40; Acts 20:32; and 2 Timothy 3:15–16? _____

_____

_____

15. In addition to giving us the Bible, God also sought to communicate to us by sending Jesus Christ.

a. Document again His identity from John 1:1, 14; 10:30; Philippians 2:6–7; Colossians 1:15; and Hebrews 1:3. _____

b. How does this truth influence the attention and authority you give to what Jesus says? _____

_____

16. When Jesus lived on earth, there was a man named Nicodemus who was aware that Jesus had come from God. He was a member of the religious sect, the Pharisees, and served on their ruling council. Since they opposed Jesus, he didn't want to be seen with Him during the day. So one night he went to question Jesus privately. Review your own questions which you identified Monday. Then read their conversation recorded in John 3:1–8.

a. What does Jesus tell him in verse 3? _____

_____

b. What two types of birth does Jesus talk about? _____

_____

17. Why did Jesus say He came to earth, as explained in John 1:11–15? _____

_____

18. To help understand the concept of "new birth," how is Jesus described in John 1:4 and 14:6? What insight does this give you? _____

_____

_____

19. Why do you think a second birth by the Spirit of God is necessary? _____

_____

How would this help with the problem of our nature? _____

_____

20. What feelings and reactions do you have to the phrase "born again," or "spiritually reborn"? Why do you think you respond that way? _____

_____

_____

21. Do you think a new birth is something that can happen gradually (that one can grow into), or do you think it has to be an "at-once" experience? Give your reasons. _____

_____

_____

22. If you have experienced a spiritual rebirth, what differences have you seen in your life? (If you have not, but know someone who has, what differences can you see in that person?) _____

_____

_____

_____

(DAY 4) Exploring the Experience of a Second Birth

23. Clarify the two ways to describe the concept of newness by filling in the blanks.

The two types of birth one can experience are _____ and _____. We are spiritually either _____ or _____.

24. If you discovered that you react negatively to these concepts, ask the Lord to open your heart and mind to His truth. Is it truth you really seek? Ask Him to reveal Himself to you and to teach you from His Word, if this is what you desire. Write your request in your journal.

25. Read John 14:20; 17:26; Galatians 2:20; Colossians 1:27; and 1 John 5:11–12. To have life, or experience a spiritual birth, what is necessary? Explain. _____

_____

_____

26. The word "believe" in the Greek connotes a response from the heart, not merely an intellectual assent. How do the following verses therefore support your discoveries above? See John 1:12; 3:16; 11:25; and Romans 10:9–10. _____

_____

_____

27. What is the result of a new birth described in 2 Corinthians 5:17 and 1 Peter 1:3 and 23? _____

_____

_____

28. Think through the above questions carefully; then write a sentence describing yourself in light of question 23. ___

_____

29. If you have experienced a new birth through Jesus Christ (either gradually or at a specific time), what were the influences which caused you to open your heart to Him? ____

_____

30. If you *think* you may have a personal relationship with Jesus Christ but are not absolutely certain, take a moment now to ask Him to come live within you. Write out your request in your notebook. Now you may know you are a new creation and have eternal life (1 John 5:13)!

31. If you have not yet taken this step, consider what Lloyd John Ogilvie says in his book *The Bush Is Still Burning:* "What we discern to be our deepest need may only be the symptom of a much more profound emptiness in us. Whatever we would analyze as our impediment may only be a sign of our real sickness. Our fears, anxieties, insecurities, and loneliness are all rooted in a need for Christ." Record in your journal what needs do you have that may be signaling you to consider Jesus Christ.

(DAY 5) Exploring Personal Responses

32. Check the response closest to your feelings:

_____ Satisfied

_____ Uncomfortable

_____ I have questions regarding this issue

_____ I would like to change my position. (I would like to become a "new creation"; or, I would like to become closer to the Lord.)

33. If you are not ready to receive Jesus Christ, review your decision periodically. When and if you are ready, complete the rest of today's lesson, excluding any questions preceded by a letter "b." If you have already accepted Jesus Christ into your life, complete the "b" questions as well as those without a letter. Record in your notebook the reasons for your present decision. Be specific.

34. If you now would like to receive Jesus Christ into your life, read Revelation 3:20 to see how you can do this.

a. Explain the symbolism of this verse. _____

_____

b. What is yours to do? _____

c. What does the Lord promise He will do? _____

35. In your journal write out your invitation to Jesus Christ, expressing your desire for Him to come into your heart or life.

a. What has now taken place? _____

b. Record today's date (your "spiritual birthday"!). _____

36. If you have previously taken this step, how would you describe your present relationship? Check below the ones which apply.

_____ Close

_____ Distant

_____ Growing

_____ Dead

_____ Exciting

37. Talk with the Lord about your present relationship.

a. If you're not close to Him, what are the reasons? _____

_____

Express your desires regarding your relationship to Him. _____

_____

What is God's promise to you in James 4:8? _____

_____

What can you do to "come near" to Him and stay there? _____

_____

b. If you are near to Him, what contributes to that closeness? _____

_____

Ask the Lord to continue to deepen your hunger and thirst for Him.

What is His promise to you in Matthew 5:6? _____

_____

38. Is this newness something we necessarily feel? What do you need to depend upon (2 Corinthians 5:17; Titus 1:2)?

_____

_____

If you don't feel close to the Lord, or if you don't feel He loves you or is hearing your prayers, is that necessarily so? What do you need to claim (Romans 8:38–39)? _____

_____

39. In receiving Jesus Christ you have received your salvation (Acts 4:12). The root word for this in Latin is *salus* which means "health" or "wholeness." What hope is there in this for you? _____

_____

40. Why is this step, receiving Jesus Christ, critical in becoming all God intended you to be? _____

_____

41. ASSIGNMENT: Repeat daily throughout this coming week, "I belong to Jesus, my Lord and my God," and "Jesus Christ lives in me!"

42. ASSIGNMENT: If you have just received Christ, tell someone who will share your joy in what you have done. Who will this one (or ones) be? _____

43. ASSIGNMENT: Share with another Christian your recommitment to Christ or a way in which you are seeing the Lord work in your life. Who will you share this with? _____

44. ASSIGNMENT: Select a verse which was meaningful to you from this lesson. Write it out and commit it to memory.

Personal Reflection (record in your journal):

1. I would describe myself prior to this study in the following ways:

2. In all honesty, my decision to receive Jesus Christ into my life is:

3. I will take, or continue to take the following steps to stay close to the Lord:

4. This is a picture symbolizing or illustrating what I am feeling now:

5. Evidence I see of God's presence in my life:

3

DISCOVERING HOW I CAN BE FREE

We may be new creations—but we still carry some old baggage! This baggage feels weighty and often bogs us down. We may wonder if we need to carry the excess throughout life or if there is some way we can be freed of it.

Truly, as God sees us now through His Son Jesus Christ who lives in us, we are new. Yet we are in process, taking on His fulness in our own natures over a period of time. This process is expressed for us in Hebrews 10:14 (note verb tenses), ". . .by one sacrifice he (Christ) *has made* perfect forever those who are *being made* holy" (italics mine).

Becoming free of the bondage of your nature is important to your becoming all God created you to be. For insight into how you can become free, turn to God's Word.

(DAY 1) Exploring the Nature of Christ

1. In the last chapter we examined some of the disturbing aspects of our behavior and learned why we are the way we are. However, when we ask Jesus Christ to live in us, we then have *His* nature within. (This is important!) Before we explore how His nature can be more fully manifested in us, let's take a look at what His nature is like. What do you discover in the verses below?

Reference	Christ's Nature
John 8:28–29	
John 8:50	
John 14:27 with Philippians 4:7 and Judges 6:24	
Hebrews 4:15 with Luke 4:1–13	
Isaiah 53:7,9 (see also Matthew 26:67–68; 27:13–14, 26–31 with 1 Peter 2:22–23)	

2. You have Christ's love in you as He lives in you. List the qualities of this love as described in 1 Corinthians 13:4–7. __

_____

_____

3. The Spirit of Christ is described in Galatians 5:22–23. List those qualities here: _____

_____

_____

4. Complete the following in your notebook: His qualities that I most desire are: (Consider questions 1–3.)

5. Watchman Nee in his book *Christ the Sum of All Spiritual Things* explains this exciting reality. "Christianity is not any one thing which Christ gives to me; Christianity is *Christ giving Himself to me* [emphasis mine]. . . God has not granted us humility and patience and gentleness, He grants the entire Christ to us." Take a moment to meditate on what this actually means. Write your insights in your notebook.

6. Why would it be defeating to attempt to develop Christlike attributes on your own? _____

_____

7. ASSIGNMENT: Examine the qualities of Christ listed in questions 1–3. Choose one of these to meditate on each day this week. Ask the Lord to give you insight into how He can be this to you and in you. Record the insights you receive and any changes you see in yourself.

(DAY 2) Exploring the Importance of Control

8. Give some examples (positive and negative) of what happens when an individual or a country comes under the control of another. _____

_____

_____

9. Read Romans 8:5–9. Describe times you have to choose who or what controls you and what are the results of your choices. _____

_____

_____

_____

10. Complete this statement in your notebook: Most of the time I am controlled by _____, which is evident in the ways I . . .

11. What do you need to do to allow the Spirit His inner control? See Romans 6:11–14. _____

How can you practically do this? Be specific. _____

_____

12. In Ephesians 5:18 we are told to "be filled with the Spirit." Charles Hummel in *Fire in the Fireplace* explains that this is a command in the *present* tense, meaning to "keep on being filled." The verb is also *passive*, meaning that the believer is responsible to be open to the Lord. It is the Holy Spirit who fills and manifests Himself in us. We, however, do not get more of God—He gets more of us! How does that help you to understand control in this relationship? _____

_____

_____

13. ASSIGNMENT: At the beginning of each day offer yourself and your day to the Lord. Ask Him to fill you with Himself and to live through you in each circumstance. At different times of the day when perhaps you may be struggling, consciously give Him control. Relax in Him. Let go—of yourself and the situation. Keep note of those times and what the results are. Also note the times when you have naturally responded with Christ's attitudes and qualities— perhaps even taking *you* by surprise!

(DAY 3) Exploring a Practical Outworking of the Spirit's Control—1

14. To help you understand how the Spirit's control works in you on a daily basis, consider the area of temptation. What are you exhorted to do in Hebrews 12:1? _____

_____

15. Why is this process important in becoming the person God intended you to be? _____

_____

16. I think of the following items when my mind turns to those things "that hinder" and "the sin that so easily entangles":

17. To see how you can be strong enough not to give in to those temptations, consider Hebrews 2:18 and 4:15-16. See also Galatians 5:22–23 and 2 Timothy 1:7. Write down your insights. _____

_____

_____

18. What additional provision does the Lord make to enable you not to give in to temptation, stated in 1 Corinthians 10:13? _____

_____

19. Record in your notebook some possible ways of escape God can provide for you in temptations. (Be specific.)

Temptation   *Ways of Escape*

20. Complete this sentence: I really don't want God's help with these temptations _____

_____

Talk with Him about each temptation. Be honest. Remember, He already knows you. Ask Him to help you want His help.

21. ASSIGNMENT: Each time you face a temptation (in thought, word, or deed) consciously yield to the Lord. Draw on His strength within you not to give in, and take the way of escape He's provided. Record those incidents and what you learn in each.

22. ASSIGNMENT: Write out 1 Corinthians 10:13 and commit it to memory.

(DAY 4) Exploring a Practical Outworking of the Spirit's Control—2

23. To further develop the practical outworking of the control of the Spirit, consider the specific area of the tongue. What description does James give of the tongue and what power does it have? See James 3:2–8. _____

_____

24. List in your notebook ways you specifically misuse your tongue: (Ask the Lord to reveal these to you.)

25. Review 1 Peter 2:23.

a. What control did Christ exhibit? _____

b. Does this mean we are never to say anything when being hassled or attacked? Explain. _____

_____

c. What does Christ's example say to you? _____

_____

26. How can Christ's other qualities (such as wisdom, kindness, love, graciousness, gentleness) help you when you feel attacked or are hurt or angry? _____

_____

_____

27. What are you told in Psalm 139:4? _____

_____

28. In Psalm 141:3 what does David ask God to do for Him? _____

_____

29. Write in your journal specific ways you need the Lord to do this for you. (Ask Him to do each.)

30. In your journal, record some positive ways you can use the tongue to help those around you.

31. In those times when you fail to allow the Lord His control, what do you need to do? See 1 John 1:9. _____

_____

What does He promise He will do? _____

_____

32. Complete this prayer in your journal: Lord, I need to confess. . .

33. ASSIGNMENT: List in your notebook the ways you see the Lord exhibiting His control in guiding what you say, don't say, or how you do say something, as you yield to Him.

34. ASSIGNMENT: List in your journal the individuals close to you. Ask the Lord to give you the words each needs to hear. Consider what each one's needs may be. Think about your feelings for them and how they may appreciate hearing how you care. Record their response.

Name   *Things I Would Say*   *Their Response*

(DAY 5) Exploring the Result

35. From the following verses, identify what Christ has accomplished for you: John 8:31–36; Galatians 5:1 and 13.

_____

_____

36. Summarize the steps to freedom described in this lesson. How is this truth expressed in Colossians 1:27? _____

_____

_____

37. Your responsibility in this is: _____

_____

38. Jesus' invitation in John 7:32–38 gives further insight into what we must do.

a. What does He say? _____

b. This passage in John was one of the most significant for Hudson Taylor, a physician, missionary, and founder of the China Inland Mission. Writing about this passage he said, " 'Come unto me and drink.' Not, come and take a hasty draught; not, come and slightly alleviate, or for a short time remove one's thirst. No! 'Drink,' or 'be drinking' constantly, habitually. The cause of thirst may be irremediable. One coming, ever drinking. No fear of emptying the fountain or exhausting the river! . . .[Then] if you are ever drinking at the

Fountain with what will your life be running over?—Jesus, Jesus, Jesus!" (From *Hudson Taylor's Spiritual Secret* by Dr. & Mrs. Howard Taylor.) How do verses 37–39 document this? _____

_____

Ways you can be "ever drinking," so Jesus Christ Himself will freely live in you and through you:

What insight does this give you into James 3:10–12? _

_____

39. ASSIGNMENT: Determine specifically how you will incorporate the above into your daily routine and record in your journal.

Personal Reflection (record in your journal):

1. Ways in which my relationship with the Lord is changing:

2. New insights I've received:

3. Questions I have:

4. Areas in which I desire continued growth:

4

GOD'S TRANSFORMING POWER

As Jesus Christ fills you with Himself, you are transformed! In Him is your wholeness. Such wholeness can be described as an integrated personality—a unity of body, mind, and spirit. You can experience a sense of this wholeness, yet continue to grow in it, until finally complete in Christ. (See Ephesians 3:18 and 4:13.)

The parable in Matthew 13:33 depicts yeast being worked through an entire amount of dough. Lloyd John Ogilvie in *The Autobiography of God* states that this parable is actually one of "the transformation of personality and, subsequently, the transforming power of a Christ-centered personality." Prior to that he says: "The person we are inside. . .will irrevocably control the personality we express outwardly to others. Any change in our personality must be a result of a transformation of the values, goals, feelings, attitudes, and self-esteem of the person who lives inside our skins. That's where Jesus begins. He can transform our personalities!" As Jesus lives in us it is His wholeness which becomes ours.

In Jesus Christ dwells all the power of God. He exhibited this power in many ways as He walked on this earth. His power and His caring are the same today. He never changes (Hebrews 13:8). In Exodus 15:26 God Himself declares: "I am the LORD who heals you." You can experience His healing and transforming power in your life today!

To discover how He can heal your self-image, transform you, and make you whole by the powerful working of the yeast of His Holy Spirit in you, turn now to God's Word.

(DAY 1) Exploring Jesus' Power to Make Me Whole—1

1. Write the phrase Jesus uses in John 7:23 to describe His act of healing. _____

_____

2. For further insight, examine an incident recorded in Luke 8:26–39. Here Jesus makes a special trip across the lake of Galilee to the region of the Gerasenes to visit a certain hurting individual.

a. Describe the man He went to see and his situation. ___

_____

b. Describe a similar person in our society who lacks wholeness. _____

_____

3. Complete this sentence in your journal: My own lack of wholeness is evidenced in the following ways:

4. What did the demoniac have or what had he done to merit Christ's reaching out to him in such a powerful way? ___

What does that tell you? (Consider also Isaiah 55:1–2 and Revelation 22:17.) _____

5. How would you describe the wholeness Jesus brought about in this man? _____

_____

(DAY 2) Exploring God's Desire to Heal Me and Make Me Whole

6. Continuing with that same incident in Luke 8, how did those who witnessed this healing and transformation respond? _____

_____

    a. Why did they respond in this way? _____

    b. What might some of their fears have been? _____

_____

7. Do you have any fears in yielding to the Lord, allowing Him total freedom to heal and transform you by His power? If so, what are your fears? _____

_____

    In a later chapter, fear will be considered in depth. But right now, discuss each fear listed with the Lord, giving each to Him. How does 1 John 4:18 help you to release these fears? _____

_____

8. Now we see we have a choice in how we respond to Jesus and in how much we will allow Him to transform our lives. What are your thoughts and feelings regarding your choice? Record them in your journal and talk with the Lord about each.

9. ASSIGNMENT: Meditate throughout the day on all the qualities of God's love that you are aware of. List these qualities in your notebook.

(DAY 3) Exploring God's Desire to Heal Me and Make Me Whole

10. Now that you have the Lord's power to heal you, do you think it is His desire to do so? In Luke 8 we saw Jesus' desire to bring healing, wholeness, and real life to a hurting person. In the Old Testament, through an incident recorded in 1 Kings 3:16–27 we can also learn more about God's desire for us in this matter.

a. How was Solomon able to tell which was the baby's real mother? _____

_____

b. God portrays Himself as a mother in Isaiah 66:13. What does this tell you of His heart for you? Consider also Isaiah 49:15–16. _____

_____

c. How does Jesus describe your Heavenly Father in Matthew 7:7–11? _____

_____

11. Is this how you've viewed God in the past? How would you have described Him before this study?

_____

_____

12. A passage in Ezekiel 16 graphically dramatizes God's feelings toward you in an allegory regarding Jerusalem. Read verses 4–14.

a. In verses 4–5, how is this person described? _____

_____

b. Yet what is God's attitude toward the one in that condition (verse 6)? _____

_____

How is this encouraging to you? _____

_____

c. What symbolically does God desire to do for you (verses 7–14)? _____

_____

13. If God were to approach you today, what do you think He would say? _____

_____

14. ASSIGNMENT: Close your eyes and visualize yourself whole, being the person you believe God would have you be. Ask the Lord to give you a vision of yourself as He created you to be. Ask Him by His power to bring you into conformity with this vision. Record in your journal specifically what you envision. Then whenever you have a moment (when you're resting or waiting for someone) as well as each night before you fall asleep, picture yourself according to the vision God has given you. This exercise will help release God's power, which is at work within you (Ephesians 3:20). (You may also practice this exercise for those you love!)

(DAY 4) Exploring Some Channels of God's Healing

15. God alone is the one who heals. He may do the healing independently, as He works within you (which will be pursued further in the following chapters), or He may choose to bring about His healing through other channels. For insight, consider the following passages.

a. John 11 records Jesus' miracle of restoring life to Lazarus. After Jesus had given him life, what did He ask Lazarus' friends to do? _____

_____

What can this symbolize for you? _____

_____

Who in your life might Jesus use as an instrument of His healing and "unbinding"? _____

b. Saul (Paul) had a life-changing encounter with Jesus Christ. But in Acts 9:10–11 someone else is called to help Saul. Whom did the Lord call, and for what purpose? _____

_____

In addition to being "a friend" could Ananias represent someone with "professional" skills? _____

_____

16. What was Saul doing when the Lord called to Ananias (verse 11)? _____

_____

17. What are we told to do in Matthew 7:7–8, and what promise are we given? _____

_____

18. Write out James 4:8 and apply it to yourself. Memorize this verse and *claim* the promise as you do the assignments below, asking God for His healing and wholeness.

19. ASSIGNMENT: Write out in your journal your requests (or simply ask) for healing and wholeness from the Lord.

James 4:2 tells us that we do not have what we want because we do not ask God. Ask Him now. Be specific, listing particular areas in place of the three dots in each sentence below. Picture yourself in His presence (for you certainly are) as you share thoughts and feelings with Him.

"Lord, please heal these hurts. . ."

"From the past. . ."

"In the present. . ."

"Lord, please free me from my fears of. . ."

"Please bring me to wholeness in you, Lord."

"Renew my mind. . ."

"Purify my heart. . ."

"Bring peace to my spirit. . ."

"In the name of Jesus. Amen."

20. ASSIGNMENT: Ask the Lord if He would choose to use another person as His instrument in some aspects of His healing. Ask Him to bring someone to mind or guide you to the one or ones He would have you talk with. Ask Him to give you a willing spirit, if necessary, to make yourself vulnerable in this way. Then do as He directs! Record in your journal your thoughts on how God may be leading you and how you will follow-up.

(DAY 5) Exploring the Process

21. As we bring our fears, our hurts, our sorrows, and our disabilities to Him, He may choose to heal us instantaneously. This type of healing is a "miracle." And miracles do happen today! Can you give an example when you or someone you know has experienced God's power in this way? _____

22. Yet from 2 Corinthians 3:18, describe another way in which the Lord often chooses to bring about His healing. ____

---

23. Describe a parallel between spiritual growth and physical growth. _____

---

24. Why is it dangerous to compare the way God is working in your life with that of others? Consider Jesus' words to Peter in John 21:20–22. What should you do when tempted to compare? _____

---

25. When will we finally be perfect, according to 1 John 3:2–3? _____

26. Does this mean you will ever in this life be whole? Is there a difference between wholeness and perfection? Explain. _____

---

27. According to 2 Corinthians 3:18, who accomplishes the growth in us? Consider also 1 Corinthians 3:6. _____

What do you think is yours to do, as you consider 2 Corinthians 3:18; and how can you do this? _____

---

28. How do you feel as you realize that God's processes often take time? _____

---

29. Personalize the prayer in Ephesians 1:17–19 as you write it out.

Personal Reflections (record in your journal):

1. Review the Personal Reflections from the previous weeks.

    a. How am I growing?

    b. What insights have I gained on the questions I recorded?

2. As I realize I can become whole, I feel:

3. Areas I am still struggling with:

4. What has helped me most in the study so far:

5. Things I'm discovering about God:

5

DISCOVERING MY TRUE SELF-WORTH

One of the first healings you may experience may be in the area of your self-image. Consider for a moment how you feel about yourself.

Do you like yourself?

Do you feel unattractive?

Do you feel like a failure?

Do you wish you were someone else?

You may be satisfied with who you are. But if you are struggling with a poor self-image, you are not alone. Dr. James Dobson in his book *What Wives Wish Their Husbands Knew About Women* writes, "Low self-esteem was indicated as *the* most troubling problem [among women he polled]." Unfortunately, this is a serious problem for men as well.

Commenting on how feelings of inferiority get started,

Dobson remarks, ". . .Your self-doubt originated during your earliest days of conscious existence." If low self-esteem has its roots deep in your past, how can you be freed from the chains of inferiority that are binding you? Can your self-image be healed or transformed? Or is a poor self-image something you must simply live with?

How you feel about yourself influences virtually everything you do. If you do not feel good about yourself, you may find yourself withdrawing, avoiding contact with others, stifling your growth, and inhibiting the contributions you could be making to other lives. After you have been with others, you may even torment yourself wondering and evaluating what they thought of you.

Dobson states that "at least 90 percent of our self-concept is built from what we think others think about us." This can become a trap, for it establishes your self-image upon impression, not necessarily on truth. Consequently you can function in life with a totally false understanding of who you really are.

Yet if you do not base your self-image on the thoughts of others, or what you perceive are the thoughts of others, where can you discover truth about yourself? What is a secure foundation for your self-image? Is there some way you can feel good about yourself apart from how you perform in life or how you are treated?

(DAY 1) Exploring How I Feel About Myself

1. Complete the following in your journal: Today, on a scale of 1 to 10 (1 being "I'm a loser;" 10 being "I am very special"), I would rate myself a _____.

2. Write in your notebook why you feel this way about yourself today.

3. Check the appropriate line: This is:

_____ the way I usually feel about myself.

_____ worse than I usually feel about myself.

_____ better than I usually feel about myself.

4. Draw in your journal a picture of how you see yourself.

5. Write out what things you like about yourself.

6. If you could change yourself, what would you change? Record your answer in your journal.

a. Of these, identify, and follow through on:

Which Can Be Changed   *Ways This Can Be Accomplished*

b. Which ones cannot be changed (those which are innate)?

7. Do you harbor any resentment toward your parents (or any other person or persons) for how you are? Be specific. ___

_____

If you do, confess this to the Lord. Ask Him to forgive you and remove those feelings, no matter how justified you may have felt about having them. Such feelings only continue to hurt you and keep you from wholeness. For any and all resentment you feel toward each person on your list, say aloud: "(name) _____, I forgive you in the name of Jesus." Repeat this as often as you struggle with resentment. Ask the Lord for His Spirit of grace and mercy to enable you to forgive. Then ask Him to heal any brokenness in your relationship with others, replacing any previous bitterness and anger with love.

8. Consider the things about yourself which cannot be changed. How do they make you feel toward God? Express your feelings honestly to Him. (He knows how you feel toward Him and understands. As you acknowledge any negative feelings, He can meet you where you are and release you from them.)

9. If you resent Him for how He's made you, write in your notebook how this has affected your relationship with Him?

10. If you are handicapped or malformed in some way, either from birth or due to an accident, how does Romans 8:28 help you? Give examples in your notebook of how you have seen this to be true in your life or in the lives of others.

11. Read Psalm 139:13–14. (Also review the verses in chapter 1 regarding how specially you were made.) Since you are a "wonderful" work of God, ask the Lord to open your eyes to see yourself as He sees you. Ask Him to give you a deeper appreciation of who He is creating you to be. Write out: "Lord, this is my request:

12. ASSIGNMENT: This week, every day when you rise in the morning say, "I'm thankful I'm *me!*" Even if you're not feeling that way, the expression takes root and helps you begin to feel that way. So, say it often!

(DAY 2) Exploring Various Foundations for Self-Worth

13. As you look around, how do you see people seeking to establish their self-worth?

14. Do you think any of these methods are satisfactory? Do you agree with Henri Nouwan that, "Somewhere deep in our heart we already know that success, fame, influence, power, and money do not give us the inner joy and peace for which we crave"? Explain. _____

_____

15. Complete this thought in your journal: Often I find myself basing my sense of worth on:

16. Read the parable in Luke 6:46–49.

    a. Considering the context of this study, what things could represent the storm that beats upon your structure of self-worth? _____

_____

    b. Review questions 13–15. Which items you recorded, if any, would be secure when hit by the storms identified above? _____

_____

17. Finish this sentence in your journal: Regarding my own bases of self-worth, the above discoveries make me realize. . .

18. What could the rock represent in Jesus' parable? _____ What do you see in Psalms 62:2; 92:15; and 1 Corinthians 10:4 regarding the identity of this rock? _____ Explain what this discovery means to you. _____

_____

(DAY 3) Exploring a True Foundation for My Self-Worth

19. Why is God Himself, Jesus Christ, a true foundation for your self-worth? Write the reasons in your notebook from the passages below, using the personal pronouns "I" and/or "me."

    a. Isaiah 44:24 and 46:3–4:

b. Jeremiah 31:3; John 15:9; and 1 John 4:10:

c. Deuteronomy 9:29; 26:18; and 32:9:

d. Psalm 147:11; Isaiah 62:4–5; and Zephaniah 3:17–18:

e. 2 Corinthians 6:18 and 1 John 3:1:

20. Complete this statement in your notebook: These above discoveries encourage me in the following ways. . .

21. Jesus, in the Luke 6 parable, commends the one who not only hears God's Word, but who also then puts it into practice. Record in your journal how you can practice the truths in God's Word examined above (in addition to the "assignment").

22. Write a paragraph: "Lord, please accept the expression of my heart to you today. . ."

23. ASSIGNMENT: Select a verse from the selections in question 19 that was especially meaningful to you. Write it out and commit it to memory. Make three copies of this verse and place each copy where you will see it during the day as a reminder. (This is a good review method for other verses, too.)

24. ASSIGNMENT: Read Psalm 107:43. Then *daily* repeat the truth of Jesus' love for you as He would express it to you, calling you by name: "I love you, _____. I delight in you. You are special!" or state these facts: "God loves me! I belong to Him. He created me special! I have worth!" (Repeat this eleven times a day, for it is said that it takes eleven positive statements to overcome one negative statement.)

(DAY 4) Exploring the Security of a True Foundation—1

25. Have you ever been disappointed with a person's change of heart toward you? Record any fears you have in trusting God's love. "God, I'm afraid to trust your love because . . ."

26. Read Psalm 34:4. What will the Lord do for you as you cry out to Him with your fears? _____

_____

27. The Lord uses His Word, His Truth, to set you free. How do the following passages help free you from your fears?

Psalms 73:21—25; 89:33

Romans 5:8; Ephesians 2:4—5

Isaiah 54:10; Romans 8:38—39

2 Timothy 2:13; 1 Peter 1:3—5

28. ASSIGNMENT: Claim one of these verses for yourself today. Dwell on it throughout the day. Repeat it before going to sleep tonight and upon waking tomorrow morning.

(DAY 5) Exploring the Security of a True Foundation—2

29. Explore further the security and depth of Christ Jesus' love for you.

a. In John 15:13 what does Jesus say is the greatest demonstration of love?

_____

At the Last Supper that Jesus was celebrating with His disciples (Luke 22:13—20), Jesus took the bread and cup of wine. He explained how these symbolized His body and blood, as He was preparing to lay down His life.

   1) Personalize the phrase in which Jesus expresses for whom He is making this sacrifice: _____

_____

   2) Whenever you doubt your self-worth, how would it help you to recall what Jesus has done? _____

_____

   b. In Paul's prayer in Ephesians 3:17–19, what description does he give of the love of Christ? _____

_____

30. How do you find yourself responding to Christ's love? Express your feelings to Him in your journal.

31. From Numbers 23:19; Psalm 119:160; and Titus 1:2, what truth do you discover that says to you, "I definitely can believe the truth of God's secure, unconditional love for me?" _____

_____

32. Complete this sentence: Hebrews 13:8 says to me. . .

_____

33. Fill out this chart in your notebook: *When the following things happen, . . .I will*

   When I start to compare myself with someone, . . .

   When I experience failure, . . .

   When I feel lonely, . . .

   When I feel insecure, . . .

   When I doubt that God could love me, . . .

When I'm down on myself, . . .

When _____, . . .

When _____, . . .

34. Why are God's thoughts and feelings about you the only true basis for your self-worth? (Ask the Lord to free you from other influences on your feelings of self-worth and to establish your true self-worth in Him.) _____

_____

35. Now that you have completed this lesson, how would you rate your feelings about yourself on a scale of 1 to 10? ___ Compare this to Monday's rating.

36. ASSIGNMENT: From John 15:9, hear Jesus say to you, calling you by name, "_____, remain in My love." Hear Him say this to you throughout the day. Think about what it means to remain in His love. Record your thoughts and feelings.

Personal Reflection (in your journal):

1. Things that have discouraged me this week and how I have handled my feelings about myself:

2. Ways I see I am changing:

3. Ways I have seen God's love for me this week:

6

ADDITIONAL HEALING FACTORS

The love of Christ can. . .

Heal you.

Free you.

Transform you.

Make you whole.

Give you peace.

In realizing how deeply, totally, and securely you are loved, you will begin to feel better about yourself. You have worth. (The God of the universe not only likes you—He loves you!) As this realization takes root in your heart, you will discover healing and a sense of your worth beginning to blossom within.

God provides His love, the counsel of others He brings into your life, and several other important factors in your healing process. To further investigate these factors, turn again to His Word.

(DAY 1) Exploring Healing Through God's Forgiveness

1. We carry guilt that can cause open sores within. For wholeness these sores need healing.* For healing, it's important to recognize those areas about which we feel guilty, and we must be honest in targeting those areas. Write your thoughts on this question: Specifically, those things for which I feel guilty (either great or small) are. . .

2. From the following verses identify what the Lord asks you to do now with your guilt, and also what He promises to do for you.

Reference	Yours to Do	God Will Do
Psalm 32:5		
Isaiah 55:7		
1 John 1:9		

3. Go over each item on your "guilt list," confessing your sin, expressing your sorrow or remorse about each to the Lord. (One way to facilitate this process is to picture each sin as a dirty package you are holding as you kneel before the Lord. Tell Him all about what's in the package and how you feel about it. Then give the package to Him. See Him reach out to take it from you. See the nail prints in His hands. Listen as He lovingly assures you of your complete forgiveness for each offense, for He has already paid your penalty for you. Watch Him blow on each package of yours with the breath of the Holy Spirit, and see it disappear—never to be remembered again! Hear Him say, "You are forgiven, my child. You are clean.") After confessing each sin on your list,

---

*For in-depth study in this area, see *A Woman's Workshop on Forgiveness*.

take some white-out or a pen and completely wipe out each item saying, "I am forgiven in the name of Jesus."

4. From the verses below, record the endorsement from God's Word of what has taken place. Personalize each passage.

>Psalm 103:10–12
>
>Isaiah 53:4–6
>
>Colossians 1:22

5. Agnes Sanford in *The Healing Light* says, "[Repentence] begins with being sorry for our sins, but it ends with joy, because it ends with a changed life."

Record your response to this statement: Having confessed those things which were a burden to me, I now feel. . .

6. Complete this sentence in your journal: From Philippians 3:12–14, I now can. . .

7. ASSIGNMENT: Write out a verse from this section and commit it to memory.

(DAY 2) Exploring Healing Through Forgiving Myself

8. Not forgiving yourself can keep you from wholeness. Cecil G. Osborne in *The Art of Learning to Love Yourself* says it is important to "begin the practice of forgiving yourself." He explains, "There are two aspects to forgiveness. One is God's forgiveness upon our confession and repentence. The other is existential forgiveness, or the cleansing that takes place when at last we are able to forgive ourselves. Most people have little difficulty believing that God forgives. The problem is in forgiving oneself." Write out a list: I have difficulty forgiving myself for the following things (I am angry with myself for):

9. Review the verses from Monday and complete this sentence in your journal: Knowing God's forgiveness helps me forgive myself in the following ways:

10. How does experiencing God's forgiveness and forgiving yourself help you in asking forgiveness from someone you may have hurt? (James 5:16 supports this action.)

How can this step help in your inner healing?

11. ASSIGNMENT: Ask the Lord to bring to your mind those from whom you need to ask forgiveness. List those individuals below, specifying the offense. Record then the person's response and the result within you, as you are obedient in this exercise.

Person   *Offense*   *Response*   *Result*

(DAY 3) Exploring Healing Through Forgiving Others

12. What are you exhorted to do in Colossians 3:13, and according to whose example?

_____

13. How Christ has forgiven you: _____

_____

14. For further insight into Christ's forgiveness, read Luke 22–23. Was there anything too serious for Him to forgive? __ The offenses you see Him forgiving, both from enemies as well as friends, are:

_____

15. Respond to this sentence: I have been hurt by or feel angry with. . . _____.

_____

16. Finish this sentence: Reasons I may not want to let go of my hurt and anger, and forgive are. . . _____

_____

_____

17. Complete this statement: The results in me when I choose not to forgive and hang on to my hurt, are . . . _____

_____

_____

18. What if the person does not deserve to be forgiven? Does that enter in to your inability to forgive? _____

_____

19. Lloyd John Ogilvie in his book *The Bush Is Still Burning* explains: "The Lord sees us with trifocal lenses. He sees with magnified clarity all that has happened to us to twist our self-images. Then He sees what we are going through now that tears the scabs off old wounds to our self-esteem. But then He focuses on the persons we can be in His image. In intimate communion He can take us back into those experiences which distorted our self-acceptance. Feeling His love, we can dare to see the negative influences of childhood and adolescence which gave us the wrong picture of our potential. Then He asks, 'Will you dare to forgive as I have forgiven you? Will you let go of the hurts?' "

Take time now to go back into those hurtful experiences. See Jesus with you. Experience His love, protection, and affirmation of you as you were then. Allow yourself to feel the pain, strengthened by His presence and comforted in His love. Open yourself to Him for the healing of that hurt. Then *ask Him to enable you by His Spirit* to forgive each person or persons involved, from your heart. Say it aloud, using the person's name, "_____, I forgive you in the name of Jesus." (Each time the remembrance returns, repeat the above.)

20. ASSIGNMENT: Go over your list in question 15, practicing the above visualization for each. Draw a line through each you are able to forgive. Record any others that come to your mind, walking through each hurtful experience in a way similar to the above example. Write down what you experience as you work through each of these.

(DAY 4) Exploring How to Be an Instrument of Healing

21. What commandment does Jesus give in John 13:34 and 15:12? _____
What model does Jesus use for what He asks you to do? _____

22. We have seen that it is Christ's love that heals and transforms. As He walked on earth, He reached out to hurting people with love, and the power of His love changed their lives. As Christ lives in you today (and reaches out to you with His love), He desires to reach out to those around you with His healing, unconditional love. To enable Him to do this, what must you do? See John 15:4, 9. _____

_____

Specific ways in which I can remain in Him are: _____

_____

23. Agnes Sanford says: "Christian love is a powerful, radiant and life-giving emotion, charged with healing power both to the one who learns to love and the one who is loved." What is one result of this love, as discerned from 1 Corinthians 8:1 and Ephesians 4:16, 29? _____

_____

24. Read the parable Jesus gives in Luke 10:25–37 and identify the details of His story as they relate to our self-image.

a. What could "stripping him of his clothes" symbolize?

_____

b. In what ways can our self-images be battered and beaten? _____

_____

c. How are the people who did the stripping identified? _

_____

d. What could the fact that they "went away" symbolize? _____

_____

e. What does the fact that he was left "half dead" communicate? _____

_____

f. Identify those who passed by. _____

_____

g. What motivated the Samaritan? _____

_____

h. In your notebook complete the two columns from the next page, describing the action he took and what that might symbolize for us today as it pertains to caring for one whose self-image has been so destroyed that he or she is barely alive.

Action Taken   Symbolizes

25. Write in your journal your thoughts on ways you can affirm and build up. . .

Your husband (or wife—or roommate if single).

Your children. (List each by name.)

Your closest friends. (Be specific.)

Your parents.

Others.

26. Lloyd Ogilvie also addresses this affirming freedom when he says: "The Lord can give us eyes to see the other people in our lives. We need their love. But most of them are so insecure themselves that there is little energy left to refortify us. 'Don't build your life on what people ought to do to make you secure,' the Lord says. 'You will always feel insecure until you are engaged in being to others what I have been to you. Find out what you can do and say to communicate esteem to them, and leave your security up to me. When you are a channel of my love and encouragement, you will know such joy that your lust for security will be displaced by the delight of cooperating with me in building up others.' When we begin to see people through the Lord's eyes, we are moved more by compassion than competition. We suddenly realize that we have discovered a liberating secret. We have been blessed by being a blessing. Security grows as we feel important to the welfare of others."

Write your response to this statement: As I begin to see people through God's eyes, I discover . . .

27. ASSIGNMENT: Identify those around you whose self-images perhaps have been injured and are "lying by the side of the road." Ask the Lord for His eyes to see their real hurts, for wisdom as to how to minister, and for His love to touch and heal them. List any specific thoughts that come to your mind of things Jesus might have you do in His name.

Individual   *What Can Do*

(DAY 5) Exploring Miscellaneous Healing Factors

28. From Proverbs 4:20-22; John 17:17; and 1 Thessalonians 2:13, what does the Lord also use to give us healing? Explain. _____

_____

What are some Scripture passages that would be helpful for you to study? (See Appendix B for Scripture to help you in times of need.) _____

_____

29. How would the perspective on our hurts, sorrows, and brokenness, given in Romans 8:28, help in the healing process? _____

_____

Finish this sentence: For me, I need this perspective now on the following things. . .

30. Some practical things you can do in each of the following areas, to help you feel better about yourself, are:

Physical activity

Physical appearance

Helping others

Intellectual stimulation

Improving relationships

Social involvement

Improving a skill

Spiritual nurture

31. Another healing action is praise. Worship of the Lord your God opens you to His fulness, bringing peace and joy within. Write out your expression of praise to Him now.

32. Read the incident in Luke 17:11–19 in which Jesus healed ten lepers.

a. Write out verse 14b: _____

_____

What does that say to you regarding the healing of your self-image? _____

_____

b. What are you reminded to do as you experience healing and growth in wholeness? _____

_____

c. Thank Him now for what He is doing within you. Claim it by faith, if you do not see specific growth.

33. ASSIGNMENT: From the areas in question 30, identify those which you feel would help you the most. Concentrate on those. Write those ideas down here along with some specific things you will do to carry them out. Then find someone who will hold you accountable for working out your ideas. That person will be (name) _____.

34. ASSIGNMENT: Put a record or tape of praise on as you are at home, or when you drive in the car. Sing along with it!

Personal Reflection (in your journal):

1. I am experiencing growth in the following areas:

2. Review the assignments from the preceding chapters.

These are assignments I still need to do or need to continue:

3. Lord, I need the most help with:

4. I am being affirmed in the following ways:

Part II

Living to My Fullest Potential

7

DOES GOD HAVE A PLAN AND PURPOSE FOR ME?

You were created specially by God.

He planned for you to be here.

God loves you deeply.

The Lord desires for you to be all He designed you to be.

By His indwelling you can be free of all that holds you down.

These are some of the energizing facts revealed through God's Word, studied in Part I. These facts can be taking root within you now, bringing inner healing and true security.

As this process occurs, you may wonder how to go further and realize your God-given potential. Considering the life He has given you, you may question how detailed God's plans for you are. Does the Creator have a general overview of your life planned, or does He intricately order your days? Is it being presumptuous to think God would take such an interest in you and in what you do? Does God really desire *you* to be a part of His great plan for His world?

Again, God's Word offers a rich storehouse of valuable truths awaiting discovery! Ask God to reveal His wisdom, knowledge, and His personal involvement in your life as you study His Word.

(DAY 1) Exploring God's Organized and Detailed Nature

1. Check the answer that reflects your thinking: In considering God's involvement in ordering my days, I feel He:

_____ Is too big to be concerned with details.

_____ Is too busy to be involved in the minute.

_____ Is the power behind the beginnings, but then lets things go as they may.

_____ Is big and powerful enough to maintain complete control over everything in His creation, in detail, from beginning to end; and He does!

2. To get a sense of God's way of doing things (thereby providing a basis for application to our lives), consider the creation of the world.

a. What sense of order is there in Genesis 1:11–12, 21?

_____

b. How is God's orderliness seen in Genesis 1:14? _____

_____

c. What impresses you in Psalm 147:4? _____

_____

d. What else do you see in creation that reveals God's detailed and organized nature? _____

_____

_____

3. What do you discover of God's planning from Genesis 6:14–16; Exodus 35:10 with 36:8–19; and Exodus 39:1–7, 21, 26, 29, and 31? _____

_____

4. How detailed is God's knowledge of you as seen in Psalm 139:1–4 and Matthew 10:30? _____

_____

5. What does Ecclesiastes 3:1 say? _____

_____

6. What does the design of your own body communicate to you about God's way of doing things? _____

_____

7. Consider the Church, the Body of Christ here on earth, comprised of all who belong to Him. The apostle Paul compares the Church to the human body in 1 Corinthians 12. What do you discover from verses 12–18? _____

_____

8. The implications of these discoveries for my own life are: _____

_____

_____

(DAY 2) Exploring God's Ordering of My Days

9. Check the description that applies to you: Up to this point, I've felt that:

_____ I'm on my own to make the most I can of my life.

_____ God doesn't care what I do, just so I'm good.

_____ God has a few major things He wants me to do during my lifetime, but otherwise my life isn't too detailed.

_____ God orders the seasons of my life and has my important decisions planned, but what I do each day is up to me.

_____ Sunday is the only day God cares what I do.

_____ Each day of my life is intricately planned.

_____ Other:

10. What do you discover from Job 14:5; Psalm 139:16; and Acts 17:26–28? _____

_____

11. How detailed does God's ordering appear from Psalm 25:4; Proverbs 3:6; and Proverbs 20:24? (Examine the words carefully for insight.) _____

_____

12. From Deuteronomy 1:29–33. . .

a. What actions portray God's leading? _____

_____

b. What phrases indicate the detail with which He guides? _____

_____

13. From Ephesians 2:10 how specifically has God planned what He has for you to do? _____

_____

14. Read Psalm 139:1–5. How detailed do you think are God's plans for you to get up, to go to the store, to make purchases, to speak to others, etc.? Give an example if you can. _____

_____

15. In considering the above passages, what do you feel the design of God's plans for your life is? _____

_____

16. Reflect on how you've seen the Lord control and order details in your life in the past. Ask Him to open your eyes to see His involvement. Record a selection of those incidents in your journal.

17. Complete this sentence: Each day of my life has the potential for. . . _____

_____

18. ASSIGNMENT: At the beginning of each day, as well as intermittently throughout the day, give your activities to the Lord, asking Him to order your steps according to His plan. Record your observations in your notebook (what you see happen, how things fit into place, how you feel within, etc.).

(DAY 3) Exploring the Quality of God's Plan for Me

19. When you think of the quality of God's plan for you what descriptive word comes to mind? _____
How does your feeling about the quality of God's plan

influence your willingness to seek it? _____

_____

20. In previous lessons you explored the motivation behind God's plans for you. In review, summarize from the following verses the truth of God's attitude toward you: Isaiah 49:15–16; Zephaniah 3:17; John 15:9; and John 17:23. _____

_____

21. Think of someone whom you love dearly. What quality of life do you desire for this special one? Consider Matthew 7:9–11. What would you conclude the quality of God's plans to be for you? _____

_____

22. Write the phrases from the following verses which specifically indicate this quality.

Psalm 23:6

Proverbs 2:8–9

Isaiah 48:17–18

Jeremiah 29:11

John 10:10

23. Check your answer to this statement: I find the fact that the Lord has good planned for me:

_____ *Difficult to believe.*   _____ *Exciting.*

_____ *Too good to be true.*   _____ *Encouraging.*

_____ *Surprising.*   _____*Confirmation of what I already knew or suspected.*

24. Why do you think many people subconsciously (or consciously) do not feel God loves them and has good planned for them? _____

_____

25. Record in your journal those things from your life (past and present) which indicate that God has good plans for you. Record anything which makes you question His plans as well.

26. Since discovering that God's plan for you is good, and knowing that He made you, would you conclude that God's plans are tailor-made to suit you? _____
What are your thoughts? (Consider Psalm 139:13–16 with Jeremiah 1:5.) _____

_____

27. Realizing you have one life, what would you like to do with it? (Think this through carefully.) _____

_____

_____

28. Talk with the Lord regarding your doubts, questions, feelings, hopes, dreams, and desires. Write your requests in your notebook.

(DAY 4) Exploring Whether or Not I Must Earn a Plan for Good

29. Your part in pursuing God's plan will be examined in the next lesson. However, here we will determine whether or not God's good plan for you is dependent on your merit. Examine the following passages and record your conclusion: Isaiah 55:1–3; Romans 3:22–24, 5:6–8; Ephesians 2:4–9; and Revelation 22:17: _____

30. What does the truth in Romans 8:31–32 say regarding your need to merit a good plan from the Lord for your life? ___

_____

31. Complete this sentence: In the past I find I've tried to merit His love by. . . _____

_____

_____

32. Explain what the ultimate good God has planned for you is from these verses: Psalms 16:2, 11; 21:6; Lamentations 3:24; and Philippians 3:8–10: _____

_____

How does this "good" overshadow circumstances? (Consider Habakkuk 3:17–19.)_____

_____

33. ASSIGNMENT: Repeat throughout the day "God is for me," emphasizing a different word each time. Record in your journal what this phrase means to you as you reflect on it.

(DAY 5) Exploring Whether God's Good Plans Means Nothing Bad Will Happen

34. For this question, mark with an "X" your reactions as you are working something through. Use an "*" to indicate where you usually end up. When bad things happen. . .

_____ I find my faith weakened.

_____ I am angry at God.

_____ I struggle with whether or not God is good.

_____ I question God's plan for me.

_____ I doubt God's control on my life.

_____ I trust His love regardless.

_____ I believe He can work all things for good in me.

_____ I rejoice in Him.

35. Does the Bible say that as Christians we will never have difficulties? Consider Psalm 34:17−19; Matthew 5:10-12, 45; John 16:33; and 1 Peter 5:8−9. _____

_____

36. Why do you think we're usually surprised when we're hit with difficulty or tragedy? _____

_____

37. In Jesus' parable in Matthew 7:24−27, which house or houses did the storm hit? What is God's promise to you here?

_____

_____

38. Write the phrases from the following verses which contain God's promise. Personalize each.

Psalm 91:1−2

Isaiah 43:1−2

1 Peter 5:10−11

39. Considering the following verses, explain the various ways that the Lord can use difficulties in your life for good, as He promises in Romans 8:28.

2 Corinthians 1:3−4

Hebrews 12:10−11

1 Peter 1:3−9

40. In light of questions 37–39, how can you help others in difficulty who perhaps do not know the Lord? _____

_____

41. The perspectives in questions 34, 37–40, can help me in the following situations:

42. Regarding His plan for you, identify the following from Isaiah 42:16:

a. What is God's promise to you as you seek to know His plan? (16a) _____

_____

b. What does He promise in 16b and what does this mean? _____

_____

c. What is the Lord's promise to you in 16c? _____

_____

43. ASSIGNMENT: Write out, claim, and memorize Psalm 138:8.

Personal Reflection (in your journal):

1. Ways my perspective is changing on God's involvement in my life:

2. Specific guidance I need at this time:

3. My perspective on the potential of my life is changing in the following ways:

8

HOW CAN I KNOW GOD'S PLANS?

Are you excited to know God does have a plan for your life that is good and satisfying, made to order for you? Yet you may wonder how to discover that plan, especially on a day-to-day basis. Perhaps you are even struggling with whether you really want His plan for your life.

Do you wonder, too, if you truly do have a choice? Are you simply a puppet, controlled by a sovereign God? Is it possible to mess up God's plan for your life? Do you fear you may have already done so? For answers, turn once again to God's Holy Word.

(DAY 1) Exploring My Free Will

1. To explore this matter of free will, read Joshua 14:6–14 with Deuteronomy 1:6–8, 19–36.

    a. As the spies reported to the Israelites what they had seen of the promised land and the people who lived in it, what choices were available to God's people? _____

_____

b. What were the results of their (Caleb's and the rest of the Israelites') choices? _____

_____

c. Give some examples of how people make similar choices today. _____

_____

2. When speaking to the Israelites at a later time, in Joshua 24:14–15, Joshua indicates plainly the choices they were faced with then.

a. What could the other gods he mentions represent for you today? _____

_____

b. What choice did Joshua make? _____

3. Why does the Lord give you freedom of choice? _____

_____

4. Consider the various areas listed below. Record in your journal any choices you are faced with in each area and reflect on what the possible results of your choices could be.

Area	*Choice*	*Possible Results*
Marriage relationship		
Involvement with family (i.e. children or parents)		
Time commitments		
Relationship with the Lord		
Direction of my life		

5. When wrong choices have been made in the past, what then? Consider the following.

a. What is the first thing to do, as seen in Psalm 32:1–5 and 1 John 1:9? _____

What then does the Lord do? _____

Confess now any wrong choices you feel you have made.

b. What can God do with our mistakes? Consider His name of "Redeemer," along with Romans 8:28 and Ephesians 1:11. _____

Ask Him now to do this for you.

c. What perspective can you start each day with? See Lamentations 3:21–23 and Philippians 3:13–14. _____

d. Write your expressions of praise and thanks to God for His unconditional love, mercy, and grace which He continually extends to you.

(DAY 2) Exploring the Discovery of God's Plans

6. From the following verses, what do you discover about your own ability to plan your life as God would plan it? Proverbs 3:5–6; Isaiah 55:8–9; Jeremiah 10:23; and James 4:13–15. _____

_____

7. How have you seen that God's ways and thoughts are higher than yours? _____

_____

8. Is there any hope for knowing His thoughts and His ways? What does God say He has given you in 1 Corinthians

2:16? _____

_____

Meditate on this thought. What implications does this have for you? _____

_____

9. Summarize what the Lord will then do for you from these verses below.

Psalm 25:14

Proverbs 1:23

Amos 4:13

John 10:3–4

John 16:13–15

1 Corinthians 2:9–10

10. To hear His voice or be sensitive to His leading, identify four keys examined below.

a. In Romans 12:1 what are you told to do, and why would this be important here? _____

_____

b. From Jeremiah 33:3; Matthew 7:7–8; and James 1:5 explain what else is important to do. _____

_____

c. A third key is discovered in Matthew 6:33 (along with James 4:2–3). Explain what this is and how this would affect discerning God's will. _____

_____

Talk with the Lord about where you are in this step.

d. Another important element is revealed by Jesus in John 15:4–7. What does this mean? _____
Why is this a key? _____
How is this accomplished? _____

---

11. ASSIGNMENTS:

a. Take time now to ask the Lord to direct your life on a daily basis, if that is what you desire. Write out your request to Him.

b. Yield to Him, giving Him the control of your life today. (Do this each day!)

c. Ask Him to refine and purify your priorities, showing you how to love and seek Him and His will above all other things.

d. Determine how you can daily "remain in Him and He in you." What will you need to incorporate into your day, and how will you do this? _____

(DAY 3) Exploring Some Avenues of Discovery

12. What is one important avenue through which the Lord can guide you, identified in Psalms 119:105 and 130? _____
Can you give an example of a time when the Lord used this means to give you direction? _____

---

13. Identify another means portrayed by Moses in Exodus 33:12–13; by David in Psalm 27:11; and by Paul in Colossians 1:9. _____

Give an example, if you can, of how God can lead using this means. _____

_____

14. Another way the Lord can give you direction is seen in Acts 8:29 and 16:6—8. Explain how the Holy Spirit can work within you in these two ways. _____

_____

Give an example of this type of guidance in your life, or explain how you think such guidance would occur. _____

_____

15. To discover another way the Lord can give you direction, read Genesis 37:19—28, 36 with 45:4—8; Esther 2:8—9; 3:13; and 4:14; and Acts 20:3.

a. How have you seen the Lord direct you by this means? _____

_____

b. Is this way always a sure leading? Consider Noah's experience in Genesis 8:6—14, and Paul and Silas' situation in Acts 16:25—30. _____

_____

c. How can you know if the Lord is leading through this means? _____

_____

16. Another channel of guidance God uses is seen in Exodus 18:17—24; Acts 18:27; and 1 Timothy 1:3. What qualifications do you think someone should have to give you guidance? (Consider Malachi 2:5—7.) _____

_____

17. How else can God direct? Consider Psalm 37:4 and Philippians 2:13. _____

As you look within, consider what desires God is placing in your heart. How is He working within you to conform your will to His? _____

_____

(DAY 4) Exploring a Specific Example of God's Leading

18. For a closer look at how the Lord can lead, consider the example of Nehemiah in the rebuilding of the wall of Jerusalem.

    a. What first took place within Nehemiah as he heard what had happened to the wall? See Nehemiah 1:4 and 2:12.

_____

_____

    b. What was the next step Nehemiah took as seen in 1:5–10? _____

_____

    c. How would you describe what Nehemiah did after that in 2:1–5? _____

_____

    d. How was God's leading endorsed to Nehemiah in 2:6–9? _____

_____

    e. Other insights I gain from this example: _____

_____

19. ASSIGNMENT: Apply the above steps to an area in which you are seeking God's will by completing the following:

a. I desire to know what the Lord would have me to do in (list an area): _____

_____

b. The burdens on my heart are: _____

_____

_____

c. My prayer is: _____

_____

_____

d. The steps I can take in pursuing what I sense to be God's leading are: (Consider the avenues studied in yesterday's lesson.) _____

_____

_____

e. Ways I sense God saying no or yes, or closing or opening doors, are: _____

_____

_____

f. Other things I see God doing to give me direction: ___

_____

_____

(DAY 5) Exploring God's Leading and His Promises

20. From 1 John 4:1 what should you do as you seek to follow God's leading?

a. How can you check indications of God's guidance? ___

_____

How have you done this in the past? _____

_____

b. Dr. James Dobson in his booklet *God's Will* lists four questions helpful in attempting to discern what God would have you do.

1) Is it scriptural? ("Guidance from the Lord is always in accordance with the Holy Scripture.")

2) Is it morally right?

3) Are the doors opening for me or am I hammering them down? (He quotes Martin Knapp as saying: "God never impresses a Noah to build an ark, or a Solomon a temple, but that means, material, and men await their approaching faith. He never impresses a Philip to go preach to an individual but that He prepares the person for Philip's preaching. He never says to an imprisoned Peter, 'arise up quickly', but that Peter will find chains providentially burst.")

4) Have I taken time to pray and think, or am I rushing things?

c. S. Maxwell Coder in *God's Will for Your Life* says, "Peace of mind should attend the doing of God's will." Peace is a confirmation that you have made the right decision and are walking with God.

21. What promise are you given in Romans 8:26–27 that is encouraging to you when you don't know what the Lord would have you do? _____

_____

22. Write the phrases beside each verse below indicating God's promise to you, personalizing each.

Psalm 25:12

Psalm 32:8

Isaiah 45:1—3

Isaiah 58:11

John 10:3—4

23. Basically, in all this, what is God's first and foremost plan for you, expressed in Isaiah 43:7 and Ephesians 1:11—12? _____

24. Complete this sentence: My desire for each day of my life is. . .

25. ASSIGNMENT: Select one verse from the list in question 22. Write it out, and commit it to memory.

Personal Reflection (in your journal):

1. What I am sensing about my life now is:

2. Ways in which my desires for my life are changing:

3. Ways I'm seeing the Lord direct my steps each day:

4. New things I've learned about my God:

9

I AM GIFTED!

Do you read this chapter title as "I am Gifted?" Many people do not feel they have any gifts at all. What is your response? Do you look at others' gifts and feel that your gifts, if any, aren't as important as theirs? Can you say with conviction, "I am a gifted individual"?

In the last two chapters you discovered that God has prepared plans especially for you, out of His love and knowledge of you. He desires fulfillment for you in your personality and life's purpose. His purpose for you coincides with His eternal purposes for the world. And you get to be part of His plan! Now life gets exciting!

As you studied how to discover God's plans, you looked at the importance of yielding yourself to the Lord. This yielding, you learned, allows Him to lead you in His way. This idea is presented by Paul in Romans 12:1–2. After he exhorts us to offer ourselves to the Lord, he proceeds in verses 3–8 to talk about the spiritual gifts God gives us. This implies that the offering of yourself is a primary step in discovering your gifts and functioning in them.

Before beginning this lesson, talk with the Lord about your feelings, your fears, your hopes, your desires, your dreams. Ask Him to free you from anything which would hinder your discovering all He has prepared for you. Ask Him to open your eyes to see, your mind to discern, and your heart to accept those gifts He has given you. Offer yourself to Him. The discovery of your gift or gifts is important. Your gifts equip you to function within God's plans for you.

Elizabeth O'Connor in the *Eighth Day of Creation* says: "When I become aware of my own gifts and give my attention to communicating what is in me. . .I have the experience of growing toward wholeness. I am working out God's chosen purpose, and I am no longer dependent on what others think and how they respond. . .I am content to be nobody because I know that in the important inner realm of the Spirit I am somebody." She goes on to say that "when God calls a person He calls him into the fulness of his own potential." Therefore, move on in the discovery of the gift(s) God has given you that help you grow to the fulness of your potential.

(DAY 1) Exploring My Natural Abilities

1. Natural abilities differ from spiritual gifts. As God formed you in your mother's womb, He created within you innate abilities. List in your notebook those abilities that you are aware of (i.e. artistic, musical, athletic, domestic, intellectual, organizational, etc.). Think of your interests, those things which give you satisfaction, the tasks which you do easily and bring fulfillment, to help you make your list.

2. Read Proverbs 31:10–31.

a. List in your notebook the natural abilities evidenced in this woman. (Her example can be applied to men as well.)

b. Do you discover any others from this passage that you also have, but had not included in either of your lists? If so, what are they? _____

_____

3. In your notebook finish this sentence: As I think through these natural abilities I have been given, I would like to further develop the following, if at all possible. . .

4. Ask the Lord to show you which ones (if any) He would have you pursue at this time. Ask Him to guide you in ways that you can develop each gift. Record any insights He gives you or avenues He opens as He leads you in what is best for you.

5. ASSIGNMENT: Ask your friends and family what they see as your natural gifts. (This would be a good topic for conversation some evening at dinner, affirming one another in his or her abilities.) Write out the natural gifts suggested to you by others. Do they agree with those you recorded above? What additional one(s) did your friends and family point out?

(DAY 2) Exploring God's Giving of Spiritual Gifts

6. In addition to natural abilities, God also gives spiritual gifts.

a. In Ephesians 4:7–8 what does it say Jesus gave us when He ascended into heaven? _____

_____

b. In 1 Corinthians 12:4–7 spiritual gifts are defined. Write out the definitive phrase in verse 7. _____

Note that one of the Greek words for gifts is *pneumatika,* meaning "things belonging to the Spirit"—not our possession!

c. When does a person receive the Holy Spirit? See Ephesians 1:13. (For further study, read John R. W. Stott's *The Baptism and Fullness of the Holy Spirit.*) _____

d. When do you think a person received spiritual gifts? __
_____

7. From 1 Corinthians 12:7; Ephesians 4:7; and 1 Peter 4:10, who does it say receives spiritual gifts? _____

8. Who are spiritual gifts to benefit, as explained in 1 Corinthians 12:7 as well as 1 Peter 4:10? What message is there in this for you? _____
_____

9. Do you think all spiritual gifts received are realized right away and are continually functional? Or can a gift remain latent for a period of time and then surface for its time of use? (Give your reasons or examples to support your answer.) _____
_____
_____

10. Complete this sentence: As to whether I have a spiritual gift or gifts, I conclude. . . _____
_____
_____

11. In your notebook write your response: My feelings about my gifts are. . .

12. Remember your discoveries regarding how deeply the Lord loves you, and that He is trustworthy and faithful. How do those facts encourage you as you approach the discovery of your gift(s)? _____

_____

13. Talk with the Lord now regarding your feelings and the discoveries of today's lesson.

(DAY 3) Exploring the Basis on Which We Receive Spiritual Gifts

14. Read the parable of the talents in Matthew 25:14–30. A talent in Jesus' day was a monetary designation equivalent to more than a thousand dollars of our money. In this parable He reveals some interesting facts about the giving of spiritual gifts and our responsibility in receiving them (which will be considered in a later chapter).

a. What do you notice about the numbers of gifts given each person? How does this make you feel? _____

_____

_____

b. From verse 15, by what standard does Jesus say these talents are given? _____

_____

c. Does it seem fair to you that some have more than others? _____

_____

d. Why do you think God would choose to give varying amounts? _____

_____

e. Is your sense of worth dependent on how many gifts you have? _____

15. Do you think different individuals deserve more than others? _____

Are spiritual gifts given according to merit? _____

What do you discover from 1 Corinthians 12:11, 18 and Hebrews 2:4 about the basis on which God gives His gifts? __

_____

    a. In Exodus 3:10–12; Jeremiah 1:5–9; and Ephesians 3:7–8, individuals are called by God to a task. What do they express about their merit? _____

_____

    b. One of the most common words used for "gifts" in the New Testament is the word *charisma* (plural, *charismata*) in the Greek. Its root is *charis,* which is "grace." Therefore, the definition of the biblical word "charisma" means "a gift of holy grace." Again we see God's grace toward us—in every aspect of our relationship with Him. What does the meaning of the word "gifts" say to you regarding any basis for pride or boasting in the gifts you receive? (See 1 Corinthians 4:6–7.) _____

_____

    c. What phrases from the following verses amplify the aspect in the giving of gifts of grace?

        Romans 12:6

        Ephesians 4:7

        1 Peter 4:10

    d. How do you think the plans God has for you influence which gifts He gives you? _____

_____

16. Complete this sentence in your notebook: My feelings now toward the gifts I may have are. . .

17. Complete this sentence: My feelings toward the gifts others have are. . .

(DAY 4) Exploring Whether or Not Some Gifts Are for Men or Women Only

18. Are some spiritual gifts "male" and others "female"? Are women eligible for all gifts, or only those behind the scenes? Give the reasons that support your beliefs. _____

_____

_____

_____

19. Does this issue raise a red flag with you? Do you genuinely want to know what the Bible says on this matter, whatever you might discover? Examine your inner reactions, record them, and talk openly with the Lord about them.

20. As we begin to explore this issue, let's first examine creation. In Genesis 1:27, how were both men and women created? _____

_____

21. What is communicated in Joel 2:28–29? _____

_____

What does the fact that Peter quoted this reference after Pentecost communicate? See Acts 2:17–18. _____

_____

22. What does Paul say in Galatians 3:26–28? _____

_____

23. Is there any indication made in 1 Corinthians 12:12–13, 27–31 of some gifts being for men or women only? (For passages which may raise some question, Don Williams' book *The Apostle Paul and Women in the Church* may provide some helpful insight.) _____

_____

24. For further exploration, identify the gifts exhibited in the following individuals:

Deborah — Judges 4:4–10

Stephen, Philip, etc. — Acts 6:2–6

Tabitha (Dorcas) — Acts 9:36–41

Priscilla and Aquila — Acts 18:2–3, 18, 24–26

Phoebe — Romans 16:1–2

Chloe — 1 Corinthians 1:11

Euodia and Syntyche — Philippians 4:2–3

25. Can you give some examples of people you know today to whom the Lord has given various tasks that support the evidence above? _____

_____

26. What is your personal conclusion regarding "male-female" gifts? _____

_____

27. Is there a difference between the marriage relationship, where the man is the head of the wife, and the church relationship of which Christ is the head? See Ephesians 5:23.

_____

_____

28. Do you think the Lord would place someone in a position that would not be in line with that person's gifts and God-given priorities? _____
Does freedom necessarily mean necessity? Explain. _____

_____

How does this help eliminate fear in considering long-range results of this issue? _____

_____

(DAY 5) Exploring Your Individual Importance

29. Whatever gift or gifts you are given through the discretion of the Holy Spirit (these gifts will be examined specifically next week), there is a profound truth that will help you in continuing to form a healthy, positive self-image. From 1 Corinthians 12:12–27, describe your own importance. _____

_____

_____

30. Using the illustration of the body, how does Paul say you are needed for the fulfillment of all God desires to do here on earth? _____

_____

How does this make you feel? _____

_____

31. What can you do when you find yourself comparing yourself with others, and discover feelings of jealousy and competition within? _____

_____

What is Paul's direction in Galatians 5:25–26? _____

_____

How does he say this is accomplished? _____

_____

Explain how living by the Spirit and letting Him direct your steps would help keep you from envying others. _____

_____

32. Elizabeth O'Connor in the *Eighth Day of Creation* has some additional insights.

> Helpful in dealing with our envy or jealousy is the knowledge that these feelings are giving us clear warning that we have abandoned ourselves. If we keep our attention focused on the other person, we only increase our pain and anxiety. Envy is a symptom of lack of appreciation of our own uniqueness and self-worth. Each of us has something to give that no one else has to give.
>
> One of the certain signs that we are at the periphery of our lives is our beginning to wonder whether or not what we are doing will be pleasing to others. Whenever we begin to act and produce with the approval of others in mind, there comes the haunting possibility that we will not live up to their expectations. To the degree that this feeling takes over we abandon ourselves, and spontaneity and creativity die in us. We enter into the sin of judging our own works, of deciding what is good and what is bad, when our only task is to be faithful over what we have—to do the best we can with it and to leave the judgement to God. We do not have to be better than others, or live up to their expectations, or fulfill their demands.

a. What is to be your perspective? What choices do you have? Consider John 12:42–43; Colossians 3:23–24; and

1 Thessalonians 2:4, 6. _____

_____

   b. Do you struggle with maintaining this perspective? Ask the Lord to truly make this your focus.

   33. What warnings are you given in Romans 12:3; Galatians 5:26; and Ephesians 4:1–3? _____

_____

What truths examined in this chapter will keep you from pride, as you remind yourself of them? _____

_____

   34. Write out 2 Corinthians 4:7 in your notebook.

Write your prayer in response to the verse.

   35. ASSIGNMENT: List those toward whom you feel some envy or jealousy. See them as one part of the Body of Christ, functioning as God intended. Recall your own importance in fulfilling the roles God has given you—or that you know are awaiting discovery. Thank the Lord for each person on your list and ask Him for His Spirit to love them and appreciate them through you. As soon as the Lord frees you, affirm them in what God has given them.

   36. ASSIGNMENT: Thank the Lord now. . .

For creating you with innate abilities:

For giving you a spiritual gift or gifts:

For giving you a special function in His Body:

For your importance in His purpose for His world:

For the privilege of serving Him:

For exhibiting His power in you and through you:

Personal Reflection (in your journal):

1. New thoughts or insights I've received this week:

2. Questions I have regarding my spiritual gifts:

3. How I see my sense of self-worth growing:

4. My feelings about my future:

10

HOW CAN I DISCOVER MY GIFTS?

Having discovered that God truly has given you a gift (or several gifts), you may be confused as to how you determine what gift you have. Perhaps you are not sure you want to know! Are you fearful about finding out what gift or gifts God has bestowed upon you? If so, talk with the Lord now about your feelings, asking Him to remove any resistance or fear and to instill you with peace, trust, and openness to His Spirit.

Turn now to His Word to begin your discovery.

(DAY 1) Exploring Spiritual Gifts

1. In several places in the New Testament, lists of some spiritual gifts are given. From each reference below, identify the gifts mentioned (listing each only once). Give if you can an example of someone who illustrates each gift—either a friend or some famous person. (One example would be

Mother Teresa, having the gift of mercy.) For definitions of these gifts, see Appendix A.

Reference	Gift	Example
Romans 12:4−8		
1 Corinthians 12:4−11, 28		
Ephesians 4:11		
1 Peter 4:7−11		

2. Some other gifts you are aware of (which are not recorded here):

3. If you could choose any of the gifts above, what would you choose, and why?

Gift	Reason

4. The gift or gifts you hope the Lord has *not* given you (and your reasons) are:

5. Star each gift in the lists in questions 1 and 2 that you think you might have.

6. In considering the gifts what is important to recognize as underlying each and surpassing all? See 1 Corinthians 13:1– 3, 13. _____

_____

(DAY 2) Exploring Illustrations of These Gifts

7. Sometimes it's easier to identify gifts within ourselves when we see them exhibited in others' lives. From the incidents below, identify the gift or gifts you see illustrated.

Exodus 18:13–24

Exodus 35:30–35

2 Kings 4:8–10

Acts 9:36–41

Acts 10:2

Acts 17:1–4

8. Having examined the gifts in others, which ones do you recognize in yourself? _____

_____

9. As you begin to discover your gift or gifts, how do you feel? _____

_____

10. ASSIGNMENT: Pray daily that the Lord would reveal and endorse His gifts to you, and give you an openness to receive whatever He has for you.

(DAY 3) Exploring My Own Giftedness

11. Before beginning this section, write out your prayer, claiming Jeremiah 33:3 and Matthew 7:7–8.

12. What gift or gifts did you record in question 3? _____

Check your motivation for desiring those gifts to see if it is honoring to the Lord. If so, the desire for those gifts may have come from the Lord and may be an indication of what He has given you. Underscore these.

13. Another way the Lord reveals how He has gifted you is through your general interests—those things that sound intriguing and appealing (for God can put those desires in your heart). Record those. (Consider also what you recorded in question 3, chapter 9.)

Things I Would Like to Do   *Gifts Needed*

Also write down any "visions" you have had of what you might be doing someday, or that you have been able to see yourself doing at some time.

Things I Can See Myself Doing   *Gifts Needed*

14. The concerns that are on your heart are another indication of your gifts (for instance, a burden for the poor).

My Burdens   *Possible Gifts Needed*

15. Another means of discovering your gifts is to examine those things you have done before. Using the categories on the next page, list the various things you have tried, and indicate if you enjoyed them. If you experienced joy, satisfaction, fulfillment, and a sense of invigoration doing something, that's a good indication you are gifted there. Consider any jobs you did because you thought you ought to. What was your response to those? Were there any differences from those you felt led into? Record any input or affirmation from others you received in the various jobs you have done. Identify the gifts needed for those tasks.

Have Done	Gift(s) Needed	My Response	Response of Others to Me

16. Considering your discoveries so far this week, what gifts do you think you might have? _____

_____

17. How does this make you feel? _____

_____

18. Write your prayer in your journal:

(DAY 4) Exploring Ways to Document My Gift(s)

19. Record the qualities and gifts people have affirmed in you in the past.

20. To further document each gift, try it out. Do so first on a small scale in a non-threatening, non-intimidating environment. Ask the Lord to provide such a situation for you. List your possible gifts; then next to each gift identify ways in which you could test its validity.

Gift	Ways to Test

21. Write out Paul's exhortation in 2 Timothy 1:6 regarding the gift(s) God has given you.

22. Having considered all this, record how you feel now.

23. ASSIGNMENT: Ask at least three people who know you well what gifts they think you have. (A function of the Body of Christ is to affirm one another in our gifts. See if you can encourage others in their gifts, too.)

People I Will Ask	The Gift(s) They Identified in Me

24. ASSIGNMENT: Pursue a situation to try out a gift, asking the Lord to open the way, or to protect. Record what happens.

(DAY 5) **Exploring My Gifts Without Fear**

25. In thinking about using your gift(s), are you feeling fear? If so, what do you find fearful? Record your answers.

26. What is it Paul says in 2 Timothy 1:7 after he exhorts Timothy to "fan into flame the gift of God, which is in you"?

_____

_____

What is Paul's discovery, recorded in Philippians 4:13? ___

_____

How do these truths help you? _____

_____

27. Do you think the Lord has given you a gift and prepared works in advance for you, only to leave you on your own to carry out your tasks? If you sense any fear within yourself, could it be this is what you are thinking? Fear would be a natural result if this were true! But what does God tell you in these passages?

Exodus 4:10–12

Psalm 44:3–8

Isaiah 55:11

1 Corinthians 2:4–5

1 Peter 4:11

28. How do Joshua 1:5, 9 and Isaiah 41:9–10, 13 help you deal with fear? _____

_____

29. Can you give an example of a time when you saw the Lord release you from fear? _____

_____

30. Complete this statement in your journal: Whenever I feel fearful, I resolve to . . .

31. Read Psalm 100.

    a. What are you to do, according to verse 2? _____

_____

    b. Who is the Lord? _____

_____

    c. Who are you? _____

_____

    d. What is to be your response to the Lord, according to verses 1 and 4? _____

_____

    e. What is the reason for such a response (verse 5)? _____

_____

32. ASSIGNMENT: Write out and memorize a verse to comfort you in fear.

Personal Reflections (in your journal):

    1. The gift(s) I think I am discovering in myself are:

    2. Ways I'm seeing each confirmed:

    3. Ways I'm seeing God's love free me:

"MY PRAYER"

Chorus: All that I have and all that I offer
            Comes from a heart both frightened and free.
            Take what I bring now and give what I need,
            All done in Your Name.

Verse 1:   You light the path as I follow,
            You free me from fears that I face.
            I live in Your love and forgiveness,
            My Saviour, I live in your grace.

Verse 2:   I take the gifts you have given,
            I see how Your plan is so good.
            Oh Lord, direct and lead me
            To use Your gifts as I should.

Verse 3:   Father, my life I have given,
            Lord, I give you this day.
            Order my every footstep,
            My thoughts, the words that I say.

Verses written by Nancy Metz
(Chorus: Unknown)

11

THE RESPONSIBILITY (AND PRIVILEGE) OF GIFTEDNESS

Now what? Now that you know you have at least one gift and have some idea of what it may be—do you have to use it? Does God care? How are others affected if you don't use your gift or gifts? What difference does it really make? To find out, turn to God's Word.

(DAY 1) Exploring My Responsibility

1. From Ephesians 2:10 what is one purpose for which you were created? _____

_____

2. Write the exhortations by each of the following verses, personalizing each.

John 15:8, 16

1 Corinthians 4:2

Ephesians 4:30

Colossians 4:17

James 2:17

James 4:17

3. Consider the parable of the talents in Matthew 25:14–30.

a. What did the servants who had received five or two talents do with what had been entrusted to them? _____

_____

What was the master's response to each? _____

_____

What message is here for you? _____

_____

b. What choice did the servant with one talent make? __

How do people do this today with their gifts? _____

_____

Who does the talent actually belong to? What does that say to you regarding your spiritual gift? _____

_____

What do you think the servant's false perception of the master shows; and what does this mean for you in your relationship with the Lord? _____

_____

4. What is your responsibility in using what you have been given? _____

_____

5. What feelings do you have about this? Talk with the Lord about them.

(DAY 2) Exploring My Motivation in Using My Gifts

6. In the parable of the talents, what motivated the servant to bury his talent? _____

7. What do you think are some varying motivations of Christians today in serving the Lord? _____

_____

8. What motivation is most pleasing to the Lord and most freeing to you? Consider Deuteronomy 13:3–4; John 14:21, 23; Romans 13:10; James 2:5; and 1 John 5:3. _____

_____

9. Complete this statement: Most of the time, I serve the Lord motivated by _____.

10. Compare your motivation to serve the Lord with your motivation to help others. What are some of the reasons you do what others ask? Which motivations are most satisfying? _

_____

_____

Relate this to serving the Lord. _____

_____

11. As you serve the Lord, what attitudes are pleasing to Him? Which are not?

Reference	Pleasing	Not Pleasing
Exodus 35:20–21, 29		
Psalm 100:2		
2 Corinthians 9:7		
1 Peter 5:2		

12. ASSIGNMENT: List ways you can nurture your love for the Lord and then how you will follow up on each.

Ways   *How I Will Do This*

13. ASSIGNMENT: List those things (big and small) that you need to do today for others and for the Lord. What is your usual attitude in doing each?

Talk with the Lord about your attitudes. Ask Him to fill you with His Spirit of love and to help you respond to others out of His love for them. Record what happens.

(DAY 3) Exploring Attitudes in Using My Gifts

14. Realizing you are a gifted child of the King, important in His eyes, what are possible attitudes or manners you might have as you use your gifts? _____

_____

15. What is the message in Philippians 2:5–7? _____

_____

16. Jesus exemplifies this attitude in John 13:2–5, 13–17.

   a. What does Jesus do for His disciples? _____

   b. Considering who Jesus is, what does this say to you? __

   c. What does Jesus tell you in verses 15–16? _____

_____

   d. As you do this, what will be the result (verse 17)? _____

_____

17. Jesus gives the same principle in Matthew 20:25–28.

   a. How does He describe His relationship to others? _____

_____

b. How does He describe the manner of other important people of His day? _____

_____

c. What is His desire for you? _____

_____

d. What rating does Jesus give the one who serves? _____

_____

18. How is this attitude portrayed by Nehemiah in Nehemiah 5:15? _____

_____

Why does he say he acted as he did? _____

19. Summarize Peter's message in 1 Peter 4:10 and 5:3. ___

_____

_____

20. Describe how this attitude is displayed as people exercise their gifts. Be specific. _____

_____

Can you give an example of one today who is a servant? ___
How can you be a servant as you use your gifts? _____

_____

21. As you respond to needs around you, whom are you actually serving? See Matthew 25:24–40 and Colossians 3:23–24. How does this realization help you? _____

_____

_____

22. ASSIGNMENT: Picture yourself working through your day with the attitude of a servant. See yourself responding to others as though they were Christ Himself. Ask the Lord to fill you with His Spirit so that you will naturally "walk through" your day in this way. To whom might you be a servant? How?

(DAY 4) Exploring How My Gifts Affect Others

23. Consider the body as Paul describes it in 1 Corinthians 12:26. How do you think your responsibility or faithfulness in using your gifts applies to this verse? _____

_____

24. Read Ephesians 2:19–22. What is your significant role within the Body of Christ? What do you think are the effects of not fulfilling your responsibility? _____

_____

_____

25. As you contemplate the needs in our world and think about God's love for each person, why do you think God has gifted each of us and placed us in unique places in His Body?

_____

_____

a. How is God's purpose in His gifts shown in Exodus 36:2–7; Nehemiah 2:4–6, 17–18, and chapter 3: and Acts 2:44–45? _____

_____

b. Have you ever observed a variety of individuals with an assortment of gifts all working together to meet a specific need? Describe that event and the results. _____

_____

c. How does it make you feel to be part of God's work in such a way? _____

_____

26. What do you lose when you choose not to do a task the Lord is calling you to? _____

_____

27. Some people feel overwhelmed by the enormous needs of the community, state, country, and world. They feel helpless to make any difference in the overall picture. Consequently they don't do anything. What would you say to encourage such people? _____

_____

_____

28. ASSIGNMENT:

a. Ask the Lord to show you the specific tasks to which He is calling you. Record what you think these tasks may be, and what you should be doing in each area.

b. Ask God if you currently have tasks for which you should not be responsible. Determine how you will step out of those areas of involvement and ask the Lord to provide the right person for that job.

(DAY 5) Exploring My Rewards

29. What is one privilege of everyone who knows Jesus Christ as Lord and Savior? See John 3:16 and 1 John 5:11–12._____

How is this privilege described by the Lord in the parable of the workers in the vineyard? (Matthew 20:1–16). _____

_____

30. Since the Lord has prepared certain works for each of us to do, what does Paul advise in Titus 3:8? _____

_____

Why do you think it is "excellent and profitable" for everyone? _____

_____

31. Scripture teaches that you will be rewarded in heaven for how you live, how responsible you are in using your gifts, and how you have allowed the Spirit to conform you to the image of Christ.

a. How is the heavenly reward portrayed in the parables in Matthew 25:21, 23 and Luke 19:11–19? _____

_____

b. How do the following verses describe the reward? Psalm 62:12; Jeremiah 17:10; 1 Corinthians 3:8–15; and Ephesians 6:8. _____

_____

c. Should this be your primary motivation? Review the motivation of the heart which pleases the Lord, as examined in question 8. _____

_____

32. What is your greatest reward, both in this life and in the life to come? Consider Psalms 17:15; 21:6; 73:25; John 14:21; Philippians 3:8, 10; and Revelation 2:26-28 with

22:16. _____

_____

What do you desire to do in response to these verses? _____

_____

33. Certainly Christ is the One to be praised and glorified in everything. Yet what does Christ say He will do for you as you sit at His banquet table in His kingdom, described in Luke 12:37? _____

_____

34. Describe your response to the Lord, expressing your heart to Him. _____

_____

_____

35. Close with the prayer in Philippians 1:9–11, applying it to yourself.

36. ASSIGNMENT: Write out a verse from question 32 and commit it to memory.

Personal Reflection (in your journal):

1. New ideas I've encountered:

2. The impact of these ideas on my life:

3. My feelings toward the Lord are changing or growing in the following ways:

4. Areas where I would like to see growth:

12

HOW CAN I BE EFFECTIVE IN USING MY GIFTS?

Help! I know I have gifts and am supposed to use them; I really want to serve the Lord. Yet there are so many needs—everywhere I turn people are asking, even pushing, me to become involved. My days already are so full—yet I feel guilty saying no to a real need.

Is it wrong to say no to an avenue of Christian service? Are there some things that are not meant for me to do, even if they're in line with my gifts? If so, how do I know? Does it matter what specific works I do as long as I stay busy and use my gifts faithfully? Will I always be effective in using my gifts, bearing fruit for the Lord, and accomplishing things of eternal value?

These are valid and important questions. For insight, turn to God's Word.

(DAY 1) Exploring Various Results of Our Works
1. Read 1 Corinthians 3:10–15.

a. What exhortation does Paul give each of us in verse 10? _____

_____

b. What kinds of material can be used in building (verse 12)? _____

_____

c. As our works are tested by God, what are the two possible results? _____

_____

d. Complete this statement: My feelings as I contemplate these verses are:

e. Complete this statement: My requests of the Lord are:

2. Explain which works are of "gold, silver, [and] costly stones"; and which can be "burned up," those of "wood, hay or straw." Consider Jesus' statements in John 3:6; 6:63; and 15:4–5. (This will be examined further later.) _____

_____

3. Paul prays that the Christians at Colossae might please God in every way. (Colossians 1:9–12). He identifies one way to please God as "bearing fruit in every good work." If bearing fruit means accomplishing things of eternal value, what is Paul implying about our works? _____

_____

4. In light of the above, what are your thoughts on the following:

"I should do everything that comes my way." _____

_____

"As long as I work real hard, I will be effective." _____

_____

"As long as I'm using my gifts, the results will be of eternal value." _____

_____

"As long as it's good, it will produce spiritual results." _____

_____

(Review these statements again at the conclusions of this chapter if you have difficulty in responding to them now.)

5. In the past, on what basis have you made decisions regarding what works you would do? _____

_____

6. Complete this statement (in your journal): It helps me to recall God's love, grace, and faithfulness toward me, and toward my efforts to serve Him, in the following ways:

(DAY 2) Exploring God's Specific Works

7. Reflect a moment on how Christ walked through His days. Consider the demands being made on Him. Consider His heart for people that were hurting and all the needs He was aware of. Describe how He handled the external and internal pressures of a day. (Examine Luke 5:12–16; 8:40–56; 10:38–41; and John 11:1–6, 17–20, 28–44.) _____

_____

   a. Write out 1 John 2:6.

   b. In your journal record what are the implications for you.:

   8. Sensing that the Lord would have us live in tranquillity, peace, and order and realizing that not every work we can do will produce eternal spiritual results, what do you discover God has done for us in the following verses? Mark 13:34; 1 Corinthians 3:5; and Ephesians 2:10. _____

_____

   9. How does Jesus' life model this truth for us in John 14:31 and 17:4? _____

_____

   10. In Song of Songs 1:6, the maiden says she was forced to take care of others' vineyards and thereby neglected her own.

   a. How does this apply to our works? _____

_____

   b. What pressures can influence people to do certain works (or "tend vineyards") other than what the King, or Lord, has for them? _____

_____

   c. What influences do you succumb to most easily? ____

_____

   11. Can you give an example of a work you did, or are now involved in, which you believe the Lord had specifically prepared for you? What did you experience in doing it? What were the results (if you know)? _____

_____

_____

12. ASSIGNMENT: Give yourself, your days, your gifts to the Lord. Ask Him to make clear what He wants; which activities you should cut back on or drop; and which activities He has prepared for you. Open yourself to His Spirit. (Review chapter 8, days 3 through 5, for ways in which the Lord can lead.)

Write out your responses to the above questions in these categories:

Gifts and Abilities

Present Involvements and Commitments

Priorities the Lord Has for Me

Possible Leadings of the Lord. . .

Commitments I should reconsider:

Areas I should focus on:

Tasks He may have for me:

(DAY 3) Exploring the Key to Effectiveness

13. Not all good works produce spiritual results pleasing to God, but He has prepared specific works for each of us. What is the key then to effectiveness? If we do the works He has prepared, are we guaranteed spiritually effective results? Look for answers in the verses below.

a. Record the phrases in each verse which illuminate the key to effectiveness.

Ecclesiastes 3:14

Psalm 127:1

Zechariah 4:6

Mark 4:26–29

John 3:6

Acts 3:12

1 Corinthians 3:5–7

b. Summarize the message of these verses. _____

_____

14. This key is clearly stated by Jesus Christ in John 15:4–5.

a. In light of the verses in question 13, why, apart from Christ, can you do nothing? _____

_____

b. What does Jesus say is key and how can you do this? _

_____

c. What is the result He promises? _____

_____

15. Jesus' life exemplified these truths.

a. What does He say in John 14:10? _____

_____

b. Who is it now, living in you, who is doing His work through you? See John 17:22–23, 26 and Galatians 2:20. ___

16. Why do you think it is the Spirit of Christ alone who can produce spiritual results? _____

_____

a. Do you think the Lord can take your works done apart from Him and use them for His good? Give reasons. _____

_____

b. Describe what results you can expect as you do the works especially assigned and prepared for you by Him. ____

_____

17. As Jesus lives in you, what quality grows in you which also contributes to your effectiveness? See 1 Corinthians 13:1–3 and 1 John 4:16. Explain and give an example if you can. _____

_____

18. How do these key ideas apply to your own life? _____

_____

19. ASSIGNMENT: Write out John 15:4–5 and commit these verses to memory.

(DAY 4) Exploring My Responsibilities

20. Although it is the Lord's work and it's by His Spirit that all is accomplished of eternal value, is there anything you need to do? From question 14, what does Jesus say you must do? _____

_____

a. Describe the difference in your life when you are remaining in Him and He in you, as opposed to times when perhaps you are not. _____

_____

b. Do you find it difficult to take time to nurture your relationship with the Lord, deepening your oneness with Him? If so, ask Him to give you a desire to do so and the discipline to follow through, to say no or wait to other pressing matters, and to develop hunger and thirst for Him.

c. What do you find are the things that most frequently keep you from times alone, reading God's Word, listening to Him, and talking with Him? What practical steps can you take to eliminate those hindrances?

Hindrances   *Ways to Eliminate*

21. The position of abiding will help you to complete your spiritual responsibilities. One responsibility is expressed in Romans 6:13 and 12:1. Why is this important in being effective? _____

_____

22. What are you told in 2 Timothy 2:15, 20–21? _____

_____

a. How can you keep yourself useful for the Lord? (Review 1 John 1:9.) _____

_____

b. Take time now to talk with the Lord, confessing what you must need to and receiving His complete cleansing. Do this regularly throughout the day as you are aware of the need.

23. Examine another responsibility in the following verses: Luke 11:28, 12:42–44; John 14:15; 15:10; James 1:22; and 1 John 2:5–6. Explain. _____

_____

a. What things may the Lord be asking you to do? _____

_____

b. How do you feel about these? For each, are you willing? Are you afraid of any? Be specific. _____

_____

_____

c. Why would it be helpful to review this lesson? (Claim Colossians 1:29.) _____

_____

d. What does the Lord say about David in Acts 13:22? Would you like to be pleasing to the Lord in this way as well? Write out your prayer.

24. Another key responsibility is portrayed in John 10:3–4.

a. As Jesus is the Good Shepherd, what is important for the sheep to do (verse 3)? (See also Ecclesiastes 5:1 and Matthew 17:5.) _____

_____

b. How is it the sheep can follow where the Shepherd leads (verse 4)? _____

_____

c. Listening to the Lord is key in knowing what it is He wants you to do moment by moment (mundane tasks as well as spiritual works). Read Scripture with a listening attitude. Keep an open ear to His voice throughout the day for thoughts that come from Him.

A tool to help you hear the Lord is visualization, or meditation. Ask the Lord to surround you with His presence and light of protection, so you will not hear anything other than His voice. Then ask Him to lead you in a time apart with Himself.

Picture yourself in a favorite spot or any pretty place—by a stream, on a rock, walking across a field of wild flowers, etc. Or you may use an incident from Scripture, putting yourself in the place of one of the characters. (For example, see yourself in Solomon's place, climbing the mountain to meet with the Lord. Or be Mary. Visualize someone coming to you and saying, "Jesus is asking for you." See yourself get up and go out to meet Him, where He is waiting for you, hoping you would come. Or take the place of John, the beloved disciple, sitting at Jesus' feet, talking with Him, listening to Him.)

25. ASSIGNMENT: Sit back and relax. Close your eyes. Take some deep breaths. Remind yourself of God's promise that as you draw near to Him, He will draw near to you (James 4:8). Know that He is right there with you. In your mind, go with Him now to your favorite place. Talk with Him about whatever is on your heart. Listen to His response. Ask Him what He would like to say to you. Record the relationship you experience with Him and anything you heard Him say.

(DAY 5) Exploring the Results

26. What is it that the Lord desires to result from your life? See John 15:16. _____

_____

In John 15:5, what is God's promise? _____

_____

27. This is also expressed Isaiah 55:10–13.

   a. Whose work is God referring to here? _____

_____

b. What are the results? _____

_____

c. What are His promises to you in it? _____

_____

28. Do you think you will always know the results of your work? Is it important to know? _____

_____

How does it help you to remember whose work it really is?

_____

_____

What attitude can be yours, regardless of apparent results? Consider Psalm 9:10. _____

_____

29. Gideon's life portrays truths explored in this chapter.

a. In Judges 6:14–16 identify. . .

Who gave Gideon the direction to do a task? _____

What was the work he was asked to do? _____

Did Gideon feel adequate to the task? _____

What reason did the Lord give as to why he would be successful and should not fear? _____

b. Judges 7 records the subsequent battle against the Midianites. Why did the Lord have Gideon go into battle with only three hundred men? (See verses 2–8.) _____

_____

What was the result? Read verses 9–21._____

_____

c. What message is there in this for you? _____

_____

30. Paul is another example of these truths.

a. Read Ephesians 3:7−9.

What task was Paul given? _____

By whose power was this given? _____

What was Paul's feeling of his own worthiness? _____

_____

b. From Acts 23:1 and 2 Corinthians 1:12, describe Paul's feelings in doing what God asked of him. _____

_____

c. Considering the impact of Paul's ministry, how would you rate the results of his life? _____

_____

31. Summarize what you have learned in this chapter. List what you have discovered to be your responsibilities and what are the Lord's. Record His promises.

32. ASSIGNMENT: Write an article about your life as someone else might write it. How would you be described? What have you done, or are you doing? What are the results of your life at this point? By whose power have you lived, and who has received the glory? Think this through carefully.

After reflecting on this, what changes would you like to see take place? Talk this over with the Lord.

Personal Reflection (in your journal):

1. I feel _____ about myself, my commitments, my priorities.

2. The hopes I have now for my life and my days are:

3. My feelings toward the Lord are:

4. Ways in which this lesson has helped me:

13

EXPERIENCING THE POWER TO BE ALL GOD CREATED ME TO BE

You have now explored many dimensions of God's healing and transforming power in your life. You have also examined the Lord's special plans and gifts for you. And you have looked at aspects which contribute to wholeness (such as yielding to the Lord and remaining in Him.)

In this chapter, some final key truths will be explored. Each is critical for you to experience the fulness of God's power in your life, enabling you to become all He designed you to be.

May the Lord bless you, manifest Himself to you, and continue His work in you, as you complete this study. His hand is upon you. His desire is the best for you. He loves you deeply. As you give Him permission, He will bring you to be all He created you to be, for your fulfillment and His glory. Open yourself to Him now as you open His Word.

(DAY 1) Exploring My Fears in Becoming All God Created Me To Be

1. Read about a man who had been disabled for thirty-eight years in John 5:1–9.

a. What was his excuse for not being well? _____

_____

b. Do you think the man had become comfortable by the pool? _____

In what ways can we become comfortable Christians? __

_____

c. There's an old adage, "Where there's a will, there's a way." Presuming the man at the pool devised ways to be nearer the stirring of the water, what fears do you think kept him from becoming whole and moving out into the mainstream of life? _____

_____

2. Even though you have glimpsed God's power, His gifts, and His specific plans for you, what fears do you have that might keep you "disabled by the pool," where all is familiar and secure? David prayed, "Search me, O God, and know my heart; test me and know my anxious thoughts. . ." (Psalm 139:23). Ask the Lord to do this for you now, revealing any fears you may have in the following areas:

Family relationships:

Time commitments:

The unknown:

Letting go of control:

The fear of failure:

Personal reputation:

Changes within:

Fear of vulnerability:

Other:

3. "Do you want to get well?" Jesus asked the man by the pool. Today, He asks you that same question. "Do you want to be whole? Do you want to be all God created you to be? Do you want to let go of your fears? Can you risk moving out of the comfortable? You do have a choice (and it's a choice you will be confronted with frequently). What is your response today? _____

4. Bruce Larson, in his study on wholeness, discovered that the ability to risk is a key factor in being a whole person. To overcome your fears (now and in the future) and learn to risk, what must you do, according to the following verses? Psalm 25:15; 141:8; Hebrews 11:26–27; and 12:2. _____

_____

5. As you keep your eyes on the Lord, what do you see in Him that frees you from your fears? _____

_____

6. To further know His faithfulness and trustworthiness, you must also hang on to His promises. Write the phrase from each verse that helps you. Personalize each.

Joshua 1:9

Psalm 34:4–5

Isaiah 41:9–10

Isaiah 42:16

Isaiah 46:3–4

7. Read Deuteronomy 32:10–11. Explain how verse 11 provides an image of what the Lord does for you. _____

_____

8. ASSIGNMENT: Every time you feel the Lord "stirring your nest" and you respond with some fear, review God's qualities and His promises. Record what you see happening.

(DAY 2) Exploring God's Power for Your Life

9. Read Psalm 33:4–11.

   a. What was made by the word of the Lord? _____

_____

   b. What qualities of the Lord are given here? _____

_____

   c. What stands firm forever? _____

_____

   d. How are these truths encouraging to you? _____

_____

10. In Philippians 2:13, what does Paul say? (Personalize this.) _____

_____

11. In Romans 4:17 Paul declares that God "gives life to the dead and calls things that are not as though they were" (as in creation). What hope does Paul's statement give you for what the Lord can make of your life? Claim this promise now. _____

_____

12. In Romans 4:21 what did Abraham believe about God? Ask the Lord to instill this faith in you. _____

_____

13. What encouragement are you given in Philippians 1:6?

_____

_____

14. The key verse for this study is Ephesians 3:20–21.

a. What can God do in you as a person and in your life?

_____

b. By whose power is all this accomplished? _____

_____

c. Who is to receive the glory? _____

_____

15. Complete this statement. My feeling as I contemplate the truth of Ephesians 3:20–21 for myself are:

16. ASSIGNMENT: Write out Ephesians 3:20–21. Meditate on this passage this week. Commit it to memory. Claim it now for your life.

(DAY 3) Exploring the Release of God's Power

17. The key passage for today is Luke 9:23–25.

a. What do you think Jesus means by "saving" your life, with the end result of "losing" it? In what ways are you tempted to do this? _____

_____

_____

b. What do you think Jesus means by "denying" yourself and "losing" your life? _____

_____

c. Explain what end result He promises. _____

_____

d. What are your thoughts as you consider the question He asks in verse 25? _____

_____

18. For further insight into this concept of "dying to self," consider the analogy of the caterpillar and the butterfly.

a. Put yourself in the place of the caterpillar. Realizing you can become a butterfly, what might you be feeling? What might your fears be? How does this relate to your real life? _____

_____

b. To become a butterfly, what must the caterpillar do? _

_____

What does this represent for you? _____

_____

c. How does the actual transformation take place? Can the caterpillar work hard enough to bring about the desired result? _____

_____

What would happen if the caterpillar chose not to make the cocoon and "die to self," trying on its own to transform itself? Explain how this relates to you. _____

_____

d. What adjectives describe the butterfly? How do these relate to whom the Lord would have you become? _____

_____

_____

19. To build on this analogy, look at John 11:38–43. What could the Lord be implying as He calls to you, "Come out"?

_____

20. As you "die to self," or "lose your life," do you think your life will become hard or boring? Will you become a person without backbone? Explain. (Consider the analogy of the wild stallion whose power is chaotically diffused; when broken his power is harnessed and channeled.) _____

_____

21. What does Jesus truly desire for you? See John 10:10 and 15:11. Ask the Lord to help you realize this truth. _____

_____

Describe what this abundant life might look like for you. __

_____

_____

22. How do you practically, daily, die to self? Explain how you might think, feel, or act in a given situation when you are living for self as well as God; and contrast that behavior with your feelings and actions after giving up your rights. _____

_____

_____

23. Explain how Jesus' teaching in Matthew 12:25 applies here. _____

_____

Can you relate a time when you were aware of a conflict within yourself? What took place in that struggle? Are you experiencing a battle now in any area? _____

_____

_____

24. Explain the difference between these two ways of living: "I'm living my life for Christ," and "Christ is living His life out through me." _____

_____

_____

25. Consider the following questions:

Are there areas of my life I am keeping for myself? _____

Are there areas in which I'm seeking my own agenda as well as the Lord's? _____

Have I released all to the Lord, being open to His plans and purposes? _____

Am I waiting on the Lord for direction and not pushing ahead with my own plans? _____

26. Express your thoughts to the Lord honestly. He knows how you're feeling, where your struggles lie, what your desires are. When you are honest with Him He can help you, and release you from whatever binds you. He understands you and cares for you. Read His invitation and promise in Matthew 11:28–30.

27. ASSIGNMENT: Ask the Lord to teach you what it means to daily die to self so that you may discover your potential. Record opportunities to die to self, how you respond, and what the results are.

(DAY 4) Exploring God's Transforming Power

28. The word for "to be transformed" in Greek is *metamorphousthai*. It means "to be transformed or transfigured by a supernatural change." It is passive, implying a yielded position—a work accomplished by a power outside oneself. This is the word used to describe what happened to Jesus on the Mount of Transfiguration. It is the same word used in Romans 12:2. Read Romans 12:1–2.

a. What does God desire you to do, expressed in verse 1? _____

_____

b. In verse 2, how does Paul say you will change? _____

_____

c. Also in verse 2, what will be the result of change? ____

_____

d. Consider the word "transformed," as explained above. How will such a transformation be accomplished? ___

_____

29. Read 2 Corinthians 3:18.

a. What is happening to you as described here? _____

_____

b. How is this being accomplished? _____

_____

30. Often Christians feel it is up to them to become more spiritual, to be more like Christ, to become all they can be. From the truths explored in this chapter, describe the effectiveness of their efforts. See also Galatians 3:1–3. _____

_____

31. What does Galatians 5:22–23 say about making yourself into a Christ-like person? _____

_____

32. In this process, what does the Lord use in our lives as indicated in John 17:17; Acts 20:32; 1 Thessalonians 2:13; and 2 Timothy 3:16–17? _____

_____

What else can the Lord use to change your life? _____

_____

33. Write out Paul's statement in 1 Timothy 4:8. Meditate on it. Give your reasons why this is true.

34. ASSIGNMENT: Repeat throughout the day these statements: "Thank You, Lord, for who I am. Thank You for who I am becoming by the power of Your Spirit! Lord, I give You myself, my life. May You accomplish Your purposes in me, and through me, for Your glory. I love You. Thank You for caring for me." Express this to the Lord in the morning, throughout the day, and before you go to sleep at night. Then watch with anticipation for all that He will do.

35. ASSIGNMENT: Record things you see the Lord doing in you and for you. Record the ways you sense the Lord is leading and for what He is fashioning you. Record any new freedom you are experiencing.

(DAY 5) Exploring God's End Results

36. Lewis Sperry Chafer in *He That Is Spiritual* comments, "True spirituality is an inward adorning. It is most simple and natural and should be a delight and attraction to all." From Ecclesiastes 3:11, what is one result of God's work within you? Explain what you think this verse means in your life. ___

_____

37. Examine Christ's first miracle, recorded in John 2:1– 10. How does this symbolize what He can do with you as a person? _____

_____

38. God's ultimate goal is discovered from the following passages: Romans 8:29; 1 Corinthians 15:49; Ephesians 4:13; and 1 John 3:2. Explain. _____

_____

39. What does God desire as we become more what He created us to be? See Isaiah 43:7; 60:21; Ephesians 1:11– 12; and Philippians 1:9–11. _____

_____

_____

40. In light of the above, write a description of yourself and your uniqueness. As Christ lives in you and works His power in you, what will you look like, and function like, in the future?

41. Record your thoughts and feelings regarding the following. . .

Whom I am becoming:

What my future holds:

Who my Lord is to me:

42. Personalize the prayer in Hebrews 13:20–21.

Personal Reflection (in your journal):

1. Ways I have changed since beginning this study:

2. Areas I still long to grow in:

3. How my relationship with the Lord has changed:

4. Ways my attitudes toward myself and my life have changed: (Look back at question 1 in chapter 5 and write in a new rating with a different color ink.)

5. Expectations I have for the future:

6. My expression to the Lord now is:

APPENDIX A

DEFINITIONS OF SOME SPIRITUAL GIFTS

WISDOM: The Spirit-given ability to give wise counsel and to act and speak in a discerning, insightful manner.

KNOWLEDGE: Two aspects: (1) the Spirit-given awareness of facts about a person, situation, or our world (for example, Jesus with the Samaritan woman in John 4); and (2) the ability to understand, retain, and apply facts and truths about God and His Word.

EVANGELISM: The Spirit-given ability to proclaim with clarity salvation in Christ and to motivate people to respond.

APOSTLE: The Spirit-given desire to go to previously "un-churched" areas to communicate the gospel and establish Christian churches.

PASTOR: The Spirit-given ability to love, care for, guide, and nurture a specific group of Christians.

PREACHING: The Spirit-given ability to present the gospel clearly and impellingly.

TEACHING: The Spirit-given ability to understand God's Word and to communicate it effectively to others for application.

MERCY: The Spirit-given ability to reach out to the unlovely and hurting of this world, bringing aid and love to them.

HOSPITALITY: The Spirit-given ability to warmly and graciously share one's home with others.

PROPHECY: Two aspects: (1) The Spirit's revelation to a person of what is to come; and (2) the ability to clarify facts in Scripture for the sake of action.

DISCERNMENT OF SPIRITS: Two aspects: (1) The Spirit-given ability to distinguish between a person or the works of God and those of Satan; also, (2) Spirit-given insight of un-Christ-like spirits in a Christian (such as the spirit of jealousy).

GIVING: The desire to give money and material possessions to others with sensitivity to the leading of the Spirit in doing so effectively.

SERVING: The Spirit-given desire, insight, will, and skill to help others in practical, tangible ways, bringing aid, strength, and encouragement to them.

ENCOURAGEMENT: The Spirit-given ability to act or speak to "upbuild," strengthen, and uplift others.

LEADERSHIP: The Spirit-given ability to govern and lead others with vision, purpose, and direction.

ADMINISTRATION: The Spirit-given ability to organize, and administrate details and business needs.

TONGUES: Two aspects: (1) The Spirit-given ability to speak another language without learning it; and (2) a Spirit-inspired "prayer language" of unknown utterance.

INTERPRETATION OF TONGUES: Two aspects: (1) The Spirit-given ability to understand what someone is saying in another language without learning it; and (2) the Spirit-given ability to understand and make known to others what another believer has spoken in a "prayer tongue."

FAITH: The Spirit-given ability to know what the Lord desires to do in a situation and to believe He will accomplish it.

HEALING: The Spirit-given ability to know what healing a person needs and to channel the Lord's power to accomplish that.

MIRACLES: The outworking of the Spirit through an individual to accomplish a variety of supernatural acts.

COMPASSION: The Spirit-given ability to respond to hurting individuals with sensitive understanding and genuine empathy.

EXHORTATION: The Spirit-given ability to see an area in which an individual needs correction and encouragement, and to help that person in an effective way.

APPENDIX B

HELP FROM GOD'S WORD IN TIMES OF NEED

When lonely: Isaiah 54:10; Jeremiah 31:3; Hosea 2:19–20; Romans 8:38–39.

When needing to feel loved: Psalms 139; 147:3; Isaiah 40:11; Zephaniah 3:17; Luke 12:6–7; Ephesians 3:17–19.

When needing direction: Psalms 25:4–12; 32:8; 37:5; 138:8; Proverbs 3:5–6; Isaiah 48:17; Jeremiah 29:11; 33:3; John 10:3–4; Philippians 3:13–14.

When facing difficulty: Psalms 37:39; 91:14–16; Isaiah 42:16; 43:1–2; Lamentations 3:19–24, 55–57; Matthew 7:24–25; Romans 8:28–39; 2 Corinthians 4:16–18; Philippians 3:8–10; James 1:2–4; 1 Peter 1:3–9.

When hurt or discouraged in ministry: Psalm 119:49–77; Matthew 5:11–12; 1 Corinthians 13:4–7; Hebrews 10:32–36; James 5:7–11; 1 Peter 2:19–24; 4:12–14; 1 John 2:17.

When feeling overlooked or unimportant: Matthew 6:1–4; 20:26–27; 1 Corinthians 12:12–27; 15:58; 1 Peter 2:9–10.

When needing wisdom: Jeremiah 33:3; Matthew 7:7–8; James 1:5.

When not knowing how to pray: Romans 8:26–27; Hebrews 7:25.

When anxious and needing peace: Psalms 46:10; 55:22; Isaiah 26:3; Luke 12:22–31; John 14:1; 14:27; Philippians 4:4–13, 19; 1 Peter 5:7.

When weary: Psalm 55:22; Isaiah 26:3; Luke 12:22-31; John 14:1, 27; Philippians 4:4–13, 19; 1 Peter 5:7.

When needing strength: Psalm 73:26; Isaiah 40:29–31; Ephesians 3:16–17; Philippians 4:12–13.

When having failed: Psalms 34:18; 145:14; Romans 8:28; 2 Corinthians 12:9; 2 Timothy 2:13.

When needing forgiveness: Psalms 32:1–5; 51:1–12; 103:10–12; Isaiah 43:25; Jeremiah 31:34; Micah 7:18–19; Romans 3:23–25; 8:1; Ephesians 2:4–5; 5:25–27; 1 John 1:9.

When fearful: Deuteronomy 31:8; Psalm 34:4; 46:1–3; Isaiah 41:9–10; Romans 8:31.

When fearing death, or grieving the loss of a loved one: Psalm 23; John 11:25–26; 14:1–3; Romans 8:38–39; 1 Corinthians 15:42–57; Revelation 7:15–17.

When suffering: Isaiah 43:1–2; 46:3–4; 53:4; Matthew 5:10–12; 2 Corinthians 1:3–5; 4:16–18; Hebrews 12:1–11; 1 Peter 1:6–9; 4:12–19; 5:8–11.

When facing temptation: 2 Corinthians 10:13; Hebrews 2:17–18 with 4:15–16.

When in spiritual battle: Romans 16:20; 2 Corinthians 10:3–4; Ephesians 6:10–18; James 5:7; 1 Peter 5:8–11.

Praise: 1 Chronicles 29:10–13; Psalms 92; 100; 111; Romans 11:33–36; Revelation 7:12.